EAGLE NEW BOOK OF AIRCRAFT

One of the fleet of Comet 4 jet-liners with which B.O.A.C. opened the first-ever jet passenger services over the North Atlantic on 4th October, 1958. The first New York to London service was flown in a record 6 hr. 12 min.

EAGLE
NEW
BOOK OF
AIRCRAFT

John W. R. Taylor and Maurice Allward

LONGACRE PRESS
London

First published 1960 by
Longacre Press Ltd
161/166 Fleet St, London E.C.4
Made and printed in Great Britain by
William Clowes and Sons Limited
London and Beccles

CONTENTS

This is Flying

AT Boscombe Down in Wiltshire is the top-secret aerodrome to which almost all British high-speed aircraft are sent for their early flight tests. Not far away is the ancient monument of Stonehenge, built thousands of years ago by people who probably worshipped the Sun. They could hardly have foreseen that men would look down one day on their great circles of stone from craft fast enough to outpace the Sun as it creeps around the Equator once every 24 hours, at a leisurely 1,040 m.p.h.

Let us pay an imaginary visit to Boscombe Down, where one such craft is being prepared for take-off. Known simply as the Bristol 188, it is a slim twin-jet research aeroplane, built to fly at anything up to 2,000 m.p.h. The sun gleams fiercely on its highly-polished skin of stainless steel, but there is nothing very unusual about its appearance. Only the more knowledgeable onlookers notice the razor-thinness of its wings, the way in which the fuselage is pinched-in behind the cockpit to keep the air flowing smoothly past at

Nearly half a century of aviation progress separates the two Bristol monoplanes illustrated on this page. The Prier-designed two-seat school machine, seen over Stonehenge, flew at 60 m.p.h. The Bristol 188 (*top*) is designed for 1,500–2,000 m.p.h.

First aeroplane to fly faster than sound, on 14th October, 1947, was the straight-wing Bell X-1 rocket-powered research aircraft, shown here under its Superfortress "mother-plane". Pilot was Capt. Charles E. Yeager, U.S.A.F., who later flew at 1,650 m.p.h. in an improved version of the same aircraft—the X-1A.

Capt. Charles "Chuck" Yeager, first man to fly through the sound barrier. During one flight in the X-1A, the aircraft fell more than 50,000 ft. out of control before he was able to level out and land it.

supersonic speeds, and the great size of the engine nacelles, all of which give a hint of tremendous power and speed.

The fact that it is so ordinary in shape is a major attraction of the 188. Other aircraft built to fly at three times the speed of sound have been freaks which could not take off under their own power but were launched like bombs from a "mother-plane" miles above the ground. By contrast, as we shall soon see, the 188 takes off quite normally.

As we watch, a test pilot clambers into its tiny cockpit, and the hood is slammed down. A stab of flame from the rear of each nacelle shows that the Gyron Junior jet-engines have been started. Their soft whistle grows to an ear-shattering roar as the aircraft begins to taxi towards the runway, and even worse is to come.

At the end of the two-mile runway, the 188 strains to break free from the wheel-brakes that hold it back as the engines are opened to full power. Suddenly, with an explosive crackle, the afterburners are switched on,

8

giving a vast increase of power by burning fuel in the hot exhaust gases. The 188 leaps forward and within seconds is roaring away in a rocket-like climb, at the start of a flight that will take it through and far beyond the once-dreaded sound barrier.

Why do pilots risk their lives by making such flights? One answer is given by the jet airliner which traces its path across the sky above our heads with a snowy-white vapour trail as it heads for London Airport. During the Second World War, many pilots lost their lives when fighter-planes suddenly began to shake violently and break up during high-speed dives. Designers knew that the trouble was caused by "compressibility" shock-waves of air built up when airflow over the wings and body of the aircraft approached the speed of sound. This was the "sound barrier" and there was no proof that an aeroplane could be made sturdy and powerful enough to fly through it until an American military test pilot named "Chuck" Yeager did so, in the rocket-powered Bell X-1 research aircraft, on 14th October, 1947.

Today, fighters like the English Electric Lightning and Lockheed Starfighter fly regularly at more than twice the speed of sound, and even jet airliners cruise much faster than those wartime fighters were flying when they were broken up by shock-waves.

This does not mean that progress has been easy and straightforward since the X-1 went supersonic for the first time. That pinched-in fuselage on the Bristol 188 reminds us of one aeroplane that would not fly faster-than-sound, although it was strong enough to do so and had a very powerful engine.

It happened early in 1954 and the aircraft concerned was the prototype of the Convair F-102 Delta Dagger fighter. Try as he would, its test pilot could not make it fly through the sound barrier. The reason was that the shock-waves and turbulent air were having a tremendous braking effect on the aircraft, and the only possible cure was for the designers to find

Area Rule. The upper illustration shows the original Convair YF-102 prototype. Below is a production F-102A Delta Dagger, with pinched-in area-ruled fuselage and bulged tail, which enable it to fly faster than sound.

a way of persuading the air to flow more smoothly past it. The answer came this time from one of the scientists of America's great research organisation, the National Advisory Committee for Aeronautics (now the National Aeronautics and Space Administration). With the help of small models in a wind tunnel, he discovered that smoother airflow could be obtained if the fuselage of the Delta Dagger was pinched-in, and if bulges were added on each side of its tail. He called his discovery the Area Rule, and you can learn more about it on page 128 of this book.

Sure enough, when the shape of the Delta Dagger was changed as he suggested, it went through the sound barrier without difficulty and designers had learned a little more about high-speed flight.

The Area Rule is not useful only for fighters or even supersonic aircraft. One of America's latest airliners, the Convair 600, has four bulged fairings on the trailing-edges of its wings. These too are "area ruling", and they enable it to fly faster than any other airliner in the world, without any control problems.

In aviation, as soon as one difficulty is overcome there are others waiting to be tackled, and there are no better places to see the shapes of the future than Boscombe Down and its U.S. counterpart, Edwards Air Force Base, in California.

At Edwards, at this moment, pilots are flying to the very threshold of space, at speeds that would have seemed fantastic a dozen years ago, in an air-launched rocket-plane called the X-15. At Boscombe, a low-powered narrow delta-wing aircraft, the Handley Page H.P. 115, is proving that the design proposed for a future supersonic airliner is safe at low speeds, during take-off and landing. Yet another research aircraft, the Short S.C. 1, foreshadows the day when supersonic airliners will be able to take off and land vertically, like helicopters. This is important, because airport runways have had to be made longer and longer as airliners have become steadily bigger and faster through the years. Today, a large jet-liner like the Boeing 707 or DC-8 needs 2 miles of concrete from which to take off with a full load, and a supersonic airliner will need even more unless it is of the VTOL (vertical take-off and landing) or STOL (short take-off and landing) type.

Research and test flying are therefore the life-blood of aviation, striving always for higher speed, greater safety and better money-making ability in the case of airliners, and better service for the passengers. They represent the most dangerous, exciting and costly form of flying; but they are only one facet of a many-sided picture.

For 100 million passengers each year flying

More missile than aeroplane, the North American X-15 research aircraft is designed to fly at a speed of at least 3,600 m.p.h. and heights up to 100 miles, where it will be virtually in space.

means a quick and easy way of getting from one place to another. The aircraft in which they travel may be a 600-m.p.h. jet-liner, a 20-year-old 170-m.p.h. Dakota, or a helicopter. The airport at which they disembark might be a £50 million architectural wonder

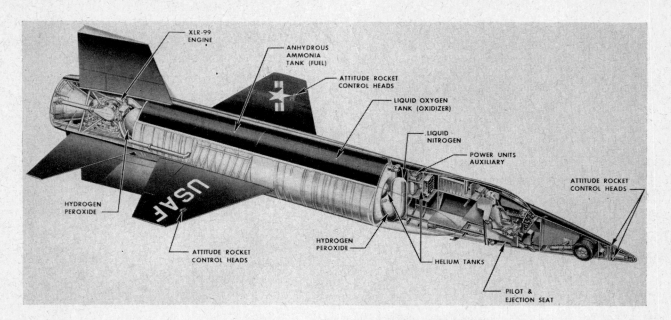

XLR-99 ENGINE

ANHYDROUS AMMONIA TANK (FUEL)

ATTITUDE ROCKET CONTROL HEADS

LIQUID OXYGEN TANK (OXIDIZER)

LIQUID NITROGEN

POWER UNITS AUXILIARY

ATTITUDE ROCKET CONTROL HEADS

HYDROGEN PEROXIDE

ATTITUDE ROCKET CONTROL HEADS

HYDROGEN PEROXIDE

HELIUM TANKS

PILOT & EJECTION SEAT

Most of the fuselage of the X-15 is filled with tanks for its ammonia and liquid oxygen propellants. At the rear is the 60,000-lb. thrust Reaction Motors XLR-99 rocket-engine, most powerful ever fitted in a piloted aeroplane. Like the earlier X-1 and X-2, the X-15 is launched from a mother-plane, in this case a modified Stratofortress bomber, at a height above 35,000 ft. It is controlled, like a missile, by movements of its one-piece tail-plane and wedge-shaped fin in the atmosphere. Tiny rocket-jets in the nose and wings take over to provide control in space. When all the fuel has been burned, engine-off landings are made on a pair of retractable tail-skids and twin nose-wheels, as shown below.

The world's biggest airport by night. In front of the glass-walled control tower and International Arrival Building at New York International Airport is an area of fountains, gardens and large reflecting pools, floodlit in changing colours.

with every possible radio and radar aid for landing in all weathers; or it might be a tiny patch of rough grass in the middle of a steamy tropical jungle. The details are unimportant. This is the everyday, commercial, matter-of-fact, money-making side of flying.

Let us go now in our imagination to Iceland and meet a man named Bjorn Palsson. He flies no 2,000 m.p.h. research aircraft, but a little 225-h.p. four-seat lightplane called a Cessna 180; yet he is as brave as any test pilot. His "airports" did not cost millions of pounds, for he flies sometimes from ordinary roads from which the snow has been swept into drifts higher than his wingtips on each side. Yet the service he offers is beyond measure in terms of money, for he runs a

Much smaller and more functional is this helicopter landing platform on an off-shore oil drilling rig. Tiny 'copters like this Hiller 12E ferry all personnel, supplies and equipment between rig and shore.

one-man air ambulance service that has saved many hundreds of lives in the past ten years.

For men like Bjorn Palsson weather is still the great enemy. Airliners have radar in their nose which can locate a storm 100 miles away and enable their pilots to fly around the worst of the weather. They have complex radio and radar systems by which they can be brought in to land safely at night or when airports are covered by low cloud. But such equipment is too heavy to be carried by a lightplane. Palsson must fly across a land of 5,000-ft. mountains and glaciers, their peaks usually shrouded by heavy cloud, with only radio beacons and his own knowledge of the country to steer him clear of danger.

In Switzerland he has a counterpart in Herman Geiger, who has landed his light-plane many times on mountainsides to pick up injured climbers. In Australia there is the famous Royal Flying Doctor Service, which has brought skilled medical attention to people living in the outback, where one's nearest neighbour might be 100 miles away. And, much nearer home, in Scotland, B.E.A.'s Air Ambulance Unit flies out from Renfrew in all weathers to serve the men, women and

Bjorn Palsson's Cessna lightplane lands on skis at Husavik, in Iceland, to pick up an injured woman who has been hauled over the snow on a sledge. Palsson's little flying ambulance had carried over 900 people to hospital by the beginning of 1960.

Top-dressing in New Zealand. By spreading fertiliser over barren hill country, spray-planes like this Fletcher Utility are improving millions of acres of grazing land for the nation's sheep-farmers.

children in the Highlands and Western Isles for whom the aeroplane is not only the modern supply-ship, but the bus to town and an angel of mercy in times of sickness.

In a hundred other ways, aviation is helping everyone, everywhere, every day. Holiday-makers fly with their cars across the English Channel. Farmers hire spray-planes to spread insecticide and weed-killer over their crops. Governments employ whole fleets of aero-planes to spray and kill swarms of locusts that would bring famine, or mosquitoes that would bring death. Police hunt for escaped convicts from the air. Coastguards haul exhausted swimmers or shipwrecked sailors from the sea by a rescue hoist on a hovering helicopter. And, whether we approve of atomic bombs or not, air forces have prevented the outbreak of World War Three simply by making it too terrible for any nation to contemplate.

So, in its myriad forms the aeroplane is being used for research, travel, ambulance service, agriculture, freight and mail carrying, police duties, war and countless other tasks. For a smaller number of people, most of them young and by no means rich, it is bringing nothing but the sheer joy and adventure of flying. These are the amateurs who are now building and flying their own little aeroplanes in every corner of the world.

As we shall see in the next chapter, they are fulfilling the hopes of the great pioneers of flying far more than are the men who build and fly aircraft which cost a million pounds or travel at many times the speed of sound.

14

These Men gave us Wings

SINCE men first became capable of constructive thought they have longed to fly. On the ground there were always enemies to fear; and the broad rivers, seas, mountains and jungles formed barriers for all but the birds which wheeled gracefully and effortlessly overhead.

As families united to form tribes and tribes grew into nations, men began to seek a purpose in life and turned to the first primitive

Flying has revolutionised international mail services; so it is fitting that almost every milestone of aviation has been recorded on stamps. Those shown here include portraits of the legendary birdmen, Daedalus and Icarus; Henson and Lilienthal; Pilâtre de Rozier, the first man to fly; Count Zeppelin of airship fame and Juan de la Cierva, inventor of the Autogiro. Famous aircraft include Ader's bat-wing *Eole*, the Wright biplane, Blériot's monoplane and Professor Piccard's stratosphere balloon. World War II stamps show Stukas dive-bombing a factory, a Wellington sinking a U-boat and parachute troops. Post-war designs commemorate Swissair's first transatlantic service and the sport of gliding.

Bladud, the British King who tried to fly, appears on this detail from a family tree prepared for James I by Thomas Lyte and now in the British Museum.

freedom on wings made of feathers and wax.

Despite a warning against high flying, Icarus enjoyed the sensation of being airborne so much that he soared too close to the sun, which melted the wax of his wings. The result was the first structural failure in history: he crashed into the Mediterranean and was killed.

In every case the wings which carried the gods and super-men were straightforward copies of those of a bird. They can be seen on carvings and statues from all over the world, from the 2,500-year-old winged bulls of Assyria to the mighty Thunderbird of the North American Indians. This was understandable. Feathered wings work so well in nature that there seemed little reason to think of alternative ways of leaving the ground. The prophet Elijah, admittedly, made use of a chariot of fire when he "went up by a whirl-wind into heaven", but there are few other early references to jet-propulsion.

Egyptian relics, discovered by archaeologists, have told us that men began trying to fly like the birds and gods before the Pyramids were built. The history books are full of stories of what happened and it is good to know that British pioneers were well to the fore more than 2,000 years ago. They had a Royal example, for King Bladud, father of Shakespeare's King Lear, built himself a pair of wings in 843 B.C. and jumped off a high building in the city of Trinavantum, which we now call London. Within seconds he crash-landed on the Temple of Apollo, and his disappointed subjects went home to hang out the flags for Lear's coronation.

Not all the bird-men came to such a sticky end. Milton relates in his *History of Britain* that Oliver of Malmesbury flew more than a furlong in A.D. 1020, at the cost of a few broken limbs. The Turks still claim that one of their countrymen, Hezarfen Celebi, flapped several kilometres from the high Tower of Galata on the banks of the Bosphorus to the

religions. They pictured many of their gods as having wings, not only because such superior beings would clearly be able to do anything they wished but because flying seemed the logical means of travel between their heaven and Earth.

So, through the years, flying came to symbolise something greater and more wonderful than the everyday world—something of which men could dream, like the psalmist who sighed, "Oh, for the wings of a dove." Legends, passed from father to son and finally recorded, told of super-men who had learned to share with the gods the secrets of flying. The ancient Greeks told of Daedalus and his son Icarus, who escaped from imprisonment by Minos, King of Crete, by flapping to market place of Scutari in the early 1600's, and have even issued a postage stamp commemorating the exploit. Nor should we forget John Damian, who tried to fly to France from the top of Stirling Castle in the presence of King James IV of Scotland. After stepping clear of the wreckage he pronounced that he would have been successful had he used eagles' feathers instead of the feathers of chickens, which are "ground birds".

With all due respect to Oliver of Malmesbury, Hezarfen Celebi and John Damian, we cannot take their claims too seriously. As early as 1680 Borelli announced that the whole idea of man being able to fly with flapping wings was absurd, because human arm muscles are much less powerful than the wing muscles of a bird, in relation to body weight. However, it can be proved scientifically that the wings of a bumble-bee are far too small to support its bulky body in flight, and even today there are many enthusiasts who believe man-powered flight to be possible.

The difference, compared with the early bird-men, is that they are using 20th-century technology to build sturdy lightweight aircraft for the job, and intend to make full use of their more-powerful leg muscles, instead of relying on the strength of their arms alone. This is nothing new, for that great scientific mastermind of the Middle Ages, Leonardo da Vinci, designed a flapping-wing aircraft worked by both arm and leg muscles in the 16th century. Between spells of painting works like the *Mona Lisa*, he also filled his sketchbooks with pictures of helicopters, parachutes, even tanks and submarines, all drawn in detail hundreds of years before they were re-invented by modern designers. But there is no proof that he built any of the aircraft.

The position, then, by the year 1700 was that men had not only been inspired by the birds but misled by them for countless centuries. When the full implications of Borelli's deduction became apparent, would-be airmen must have been terribly depressed,

for what possible alternative to flapping wings could be imagined?

In fact, as we know now, there were at least four lines of development left to the pioneers: fixed-wing (aeroplane), rotating-wing (helicopter), mechanical flapping-wing (ornithopter) and lighter-than-air (balloon and airship). All had been tried at some time or other. For example, Archytas of Tarentum is supposed to have built a successful "flying pigeon" in the 5th century B.C., while the Chinese aerial spinning top and kite were primitive forms of helicopter and aeroplane respectively.

The snag with most forms of flying machine, except the balloon, was that they required some form of engine. Even the steam engine in a really practical form was still some years away and it was never to prove light enough in weight for efficient use in an aeroplane. So the only hope lay in some form of lighter-than-air craft.

The story of real flying can therefore be said to have started in the 13th century, when a British monk named Roger Bacon expressed the theory that air was an invisible fluid, and that if an object were made lighter than air it would float on the aerial ocean just as a ship

Unlike most bird-men, the French locksmith Besnier planned to use both arms and legs to work his 1678 version of the flapping wings with which brave men had been jumping off high buildings for years.

21st November, 1783. The first aerial journey. Pilâtre de Rozier and the Marquis d'Arlandes in a Montgolfier balloon.

floats on water. It is claimed that he tried to prove his point by designing a copper cylinder which would float when filled with hot air. If he did, it showed remarkable foresight, for when the first successful piloted aircraft was built 500 years later it was, in fact, a hot-air balloon.

In the intervening years there is no record of anybody being aware that hot air rises, because it is lighter than cold air, and might therefore be used to raise an aircraft off the ground. But there was no shortage of alternative suggestions.

The prize for ingenuity must go to Gaspard Schott, who suggested that dew rose from the grass after sunrise and that, consequently, if empty eggshells were filled with dew they would take off as soon as the sun shone on them.

More sensible was de Lana's famous Flying Boat, designed in 1670, which consisted of a boat-shaped car slung under four large copper globes. De Lana hoped to make the whole thing lighter-than-air by creating a vacuum inside each globe, and his theories were supported by several leading physicists of his day. Others proved conclusively that the globes could never be made sufficiently big and light to achieve both buoyancy and sufficient strength to withstand outside pressure—a fact which may have helped de Lana decide not to go ahead with his Flying Boat "in case it were used to drop fire-balls on soldiers and cities in time of war".

Then, in 1766, an English chemist named Henry Cavendish managed to isolate a new gas named hydrogen, and the centuries-old quest for a lifting-force was over, for it proved to be lighter than air. The importance of his discovery was not realised for some time, and meanwhile things were happening in France.

It seems that one day the brothers Joseph and Etienne Montgolfier, paper-makers of Annonay, near Lyons, were sitting at home by the fire, watching the smoke curling upwards. They decided to see if it was strong enough to lift a paper bag. It was! Excitedly they made a larger bag of fine silk and found that this too rose when paper was burned under its open end. The larger they built their *balons*, the better they flew. So before long they decided to let the public into their secret, and announced that on 5th June, 1783, they would demonstrate a 110-ft. diameter fire-balloon made of paper-lined linen.

Accustomed to the exploits of would-be aeronauts, a crowd gathered with the intention of having some harmless fun at the expense of the Montgolfiers rather than with any real hope of seeing history made. But when a fire

THE STORY OF BALLOONS AND AIRSHIPS

The earliest complete design for a lighter-than-air craft was de Lana's Aerial Ship of 1670 (*centre*). In 1782 Joseph and Etienne Montgolfier discovered that hot air rising from a fire would lift a paper bag.

A sheep, cock and duck were the first passengers in a Montgolfier balloon in 1783 (*left*). More safe was Charles' hydrogen-filled balloon (*centre*), and Vincent Lunardi made the first aerial voyage in Britain in a craft of this type in 1784 (*right*).

First successful parachute descent was made by Jacques Garnerin over Paris in 1797 (*left*). First British design for an airship was Martyn's Aerostatic Globe of 1783 (*centre*). Sir George Cayley was first to advocate a streamlined gas-bag, on his 1837 steam-driven airship project (*right*).

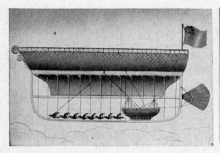

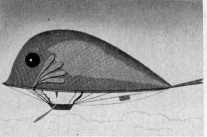

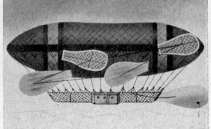

Mackintosh's flying ship (*left*) was to be drawn by 16 eagles. Other fanciful projects included Pauly and Egg's *Dolphin* of 1816 (*centre*) and Lennox's *Eagle* (*right*) which was designed to link the capitals of Europe in 1835, but never flew.

19

7th January, 1785. Blanchard and Jeffries make the first aerial crossing of the Channel in a hydrogen balloon. Note the silk-covered oars, which were of course quite useless, as was Blanchard's later "moulinet"—a hand-operated fan which foreshadowed the propeller.

greatest test was still to come. Could the balloon be used for human flight?

As it turned out, the first aeronauts were not human, for when the Montgolfiers demonstrated their first passenger-carrying balloon, they bestowed that rather dubious honour on a sheep, a cock and a duck, which they encaged in a wicker basket slung under the balloon. The animals suffered no ill effects, and it was next proposed to replace them with a condemned convict; but a young scientist named Pilâtre de Rozier decided that this would not be a happy start for the new science of flight, and volunteered for the job himself. So, on 15th October, 1783, he became the first man in the world to "fly", in a huge, gaudy *Montgolfière*, which was securely roped to the ground to make sure it did not go too far! One month later, on 21st November, he made the first aerial voyage in history, by flying 5½ miles over Paris with the Marquis d'Arlandes.

There is little doubt of the courage of de Rozier and his passenger, for they were able to keep airborne only by stoking the fire under their balloon, a task which had to be interrupted frequently to put out other fires which broke out on the fabric of the balloon itself. But safer balloons were on the way, and on 1st December, 1783, Professor Charles, another Frenchman, made a flight of 27 miles in a hydrogen-filled balloon built by two brothers named Robert. It was such a first-class aircraft that its basic design has remained standard for almost every balloon built since. In particular, the hydrogen was contained inside a sealed "bag", so that flight could be maintained for as long as the aeronaut wished and ended simply by releasing some of the gas through a valve.

News of these French successes spread quickly and *Montgolfières* and *Charlières* were soon flying in many countries. The first brief ascent in Britain was made at Edinburgh, on 25th August, 1784, by James Tytler. Five months later, on 7th January, 1785, the French

was lit under the balloon, creating so much lift that eight men were needed to hold it down, it was apparent that something spectacular was about to happen. At a signal from the Montgolfiers, the ropes were released and the balloon shot up to 6,000 ft., travelling downwind more than a mile before the air cooled and it sank to the ground. So, after countless centuries of effort and heartbreak, the air had at last been conquered—but the balloonist Blanchard completed the first aerial crossing of the Channel, accompanied by the wealthy American, Dr. John Jeffries.

The story of their flight is one of the most exciting and amusing in the history of flying. At one stage they lost height so rapidly that they almost skimmed the waves and had to throw overboard everything they could lay their hands on to lighten the balloon. Even then they would not have reached land but for a sudden gust of wind which carried them up, over the French coast, where they landed minus even their clothes!

It is doubtful if the British Government of the time realised the full significance of this pioneer flight over England's "moat"; but Napoleon did, and twenty years later seriously considered invading England with the help of giant *Montgolfières*, each carrying 3,000 troops. This particular idea came to nothing, but the balloon entered military service as early as 1794, when a captive one was used for observation duties during the Battle of Fleurus, contributing greatly to the French victory. However, the chief use of the balloon continued to be for pleasure, and the sport was given a new lease of life when Charles Green discovered that coal gas, which was available in large quantities following its introduction to light streets in London in 1807, was a good substitute for the expensive hydrogen.

Green himself made the most publicised long-distance flight of the century when he flew in 1836 from Vauxhall Gardens, London, to Weilburg in Germany, a distance of nearly 500 miles. But despite a few such outstanding journeys, the limitations of the free balloon as a means of air travel had been obvious from the start, and, apart from some scientific and military applications, ballooning never developed into much more than a hazardous sport.

The two requirements for turning the balloon into a practical vehicle were to find a method of steering it, so that it did not always have to travel precisely down-wind, and some

form of engine to propel it even against a head-wind. The man who pointed the way to an answer was a great Yorkshireman named Sir George Cayley.

Cayley is often called "the Father of Aerial Navigation", and it is a well-deserved title because he discovered the basic principles of aeronautics that led in turn to both the navigable balloon and the aeroplane.

One of his earliest inventions was an improved Chinese flying top, which proved that considerable lift and, consequently, thrust could be obtained from an efficient airscrew. Then, in 1804, Cayley built the first practical glider. It was little more than a kite with a cruciform tail, but it established the relative

Invasion of England. These giant *Montgolfières*, each intended to carry 3,000 of Napoleon's soldiers, were never built, but represent the first planned use of aircraft for military attack.

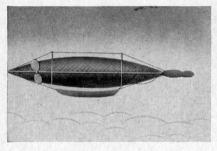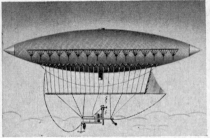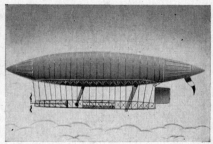

Three of the most important milestones in the development of the airship. Jullien's clockwork-driven *Précurseur* of 1850 (*left*) was the earliest successful model airship. It paved the way for Giffard's full-size steam-powered airship (*centre*), which flew from Paris to Trappes in 1852. First completely practical airship, able to be steered in flight, was the electrically-driven *La France* (*right*) of Renard and Krebs, in 1884.

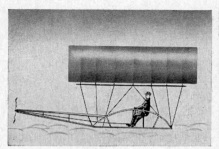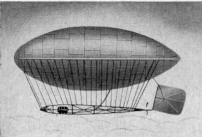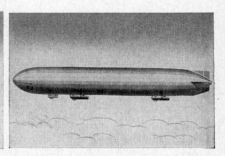

Ritchell's Sky Bicycle (*left*) attempted to avoid complicated power-plants by use of a pedal-driven propeller. Better known is Santos-Dumont's airship (*centre*) in which he flew round the Eiffel Tower in Paris in 1901. By then the first military airships were being built in Europe, and German Zeppelins (*right*) not only operated the world's first airline services but became the first long-range bombers of the 1914–18 War.

positions of wing and tail units as on modern aircraft: and it flew. It was scaled-up later into a glider bigger than an Auster, and it was in this aircraft that Cayley is supposed to have flown his reluctant coachman 300 yards across a valley, after which the man resigned on the spot!

Whether or not that story is true, there is no doubt of Cayley's great contribution to the progress of flight. By studying the birds, he deduced that aircraft wings ought to be cambered, adding that a braced biplane arrangement would combine high lift with structural strength. He even designed an aircraft to prove his theories, but seems to have abandoned it in favour of hydrogen-filled airships, which he regarded as more suitable

for extensive air travel. He emphasised the need for streamlining the envelope, but was prevented from advancing any further by lack of a suitable engine.

For a whole century after Pilâtre de Rozier's pioneer flight in a balloon it was this engine problem which hampered progress. As early as 1784 Blanchard had tried to propel a balloon with a revolving fan, while two other Frenchmen named Miolan and Janinet attempted to drive a *Montgolfière* by jets of hot air from inside the balloon—a primitive form of jet-propulsion. But it was not until Pierre Jullien flew his clockwork-powered streamlined model airship *Le Précurseur* in 1850 that any real headway was made. Within two years Henri Giffard flew from Paris to Trappes at the reckless speed of 6 m.p.h. in a partly controllable full-size airship on similar lines, fitted with a 3-h.p. steam engine. By 1872 the record had been raised to 10 m.p.h., by Paul Haenlein, a German, whose airship was driven by an engine fed with gas from the envelope. Professor Ritchell in America preferred man-power, and caused a lot of excitement with his *Sky Bicycle*, a small airship propelled by a pedal-driven propeller. But the first completely successful airship was the electrically driven *La France*, built in 1884 by Renard and Krebs, as it was the first that could be steered in flight back to its starting-point, irrespective of wind.

Then, at last, came the invention for which everyone had been waiting since Borelli had shown the inadequacy of muscle-power for flight—the internal-combustion engine. The man primarily responsible was Dr. N. A. Otto of Germany, who produced his famous four-stroke "silent gas engine" in 1876. For the first ten years engines of this kind were still not suitable for aircraft, because they weighed as much as 1,100 lb. per h.p. and ran at only 200 revolutions per minute. Another German, Gottlieb Daimler, then came on the scene and adapted the Otto type of engine to run on "petrol" fuels at a full 800 rev. per minute. This brought down the power-to-weight figure to 88 lb. per h.p., and the power for flight was finally available.

Inevitably, it was in the airship that the petrol engine first made history, and the man of the moment was Alberto Santos-Dumont, a dapper, courageous, little Brazilian who lived in France. He won 100,000 francs and became the idol of Paris when he made the first flight around the Eiffel Tower in one of his tiny airships in 1901. Later he demonstrated the possibilities of flying by using an airship just like a cab for travelling to town, leaving it tied down outside his club in Paris while he had lunch.

Nowadays we look back on such exploits with almost as much amazement as they caused at the time. For better or for worse, the baby airship was overshadowed completely within a few years by the fixed-wing aeroplane, which did not share its ability to take off and land vertically. Operation into city centres became completely impractical and today we often have to spend the best part of an hour riding in a motor coach from city-centre to airport before we can even begin a journey by air. At the same time, we are searching for new types of VTO (vertical take-off) aircraft to make possible what Santos-Dumont was able to do some sixty years ago.

Big airships continued to be developed, particularly by Count Ferdinand von Zeppelin of Germany. Unlike Santos-Dumont's aircraft, in which the envelope, or gas-bag, was filled out by the gas inside it, the Zeppelins were rigid airships. Their outer covering was stretched over a metal frame, and the hydrogen lifting gas was contained in smaller gas-bags inside this structure. During the 1914–18 War they spearheaded Germany's bombing raids on Britain and met with considerable success until the evolution of the first night-fighter aeroplanes brought their career to an end.

Even then, there remained the hope that the big rigid airship might rival the fixed-wing airliner for passenger-carrying over long distances. The very first airline services had been operated by the Zeppelin company between Lake Constance and Berlin in 1910, when the average aeroplane was a frail, unreliable contraption of stick-and-canvas. By the outbreak of war in 1914, using a total of six Zeppelins, they had carried 35,000 passengers; and the prospects for airship travel seemed even brighter in 1919 when the British R.34 made the first two-way air crossing of the North Atlantic.

Once again, it was left to Germany to set the pace, and the wonderful old *Graf Zeppelin* completed in 1928, will always be remembered as one of the greatest aircraft ever built. She was great in size, with a length of 772 ft., diameter of 100 ft., five engines developing a

Inside the Zeppelins

Few people remember nowadays that German Zeppelin airships operated regular passenger services across the Atlantic long before aeroplanes were capable of doing so. Nor is it generally realised what a high standard of comfort was offered by these giants of the sky.

A voyage on board the *Graf Zeppelin* or *Hindenburg* combined something of the luxury and adventure of sea travel with the speed of air travel. A journey in the *Hindenburg* from Frankfurt to the United States took just over $2\frac{1}{2}$ days, according to the weather. Up to fifty passengers were carried, at a fare of £53. There were lounges, with room to dance, a dining saloon, smoking room, promenade decks, an orchestra—everything found on an ocean liner except a swimming pool.

Anyone accustomed to the confined cabins of even the largest modern airliner must find it difficult to believe that the pictures on this page were taken on board transatlantic aircraft of a quarter of a century ago; but they were. At the top is the control car of the *Hindenburg*. Underneath it are scenes inside the lounge of the *Graf Zeppelin* (*centre*) and the dining-room of the *Hindenburg* (*bottom left*). The other picture (*below right*) was taken in one of the passenger cabins, equipped with two bunks.

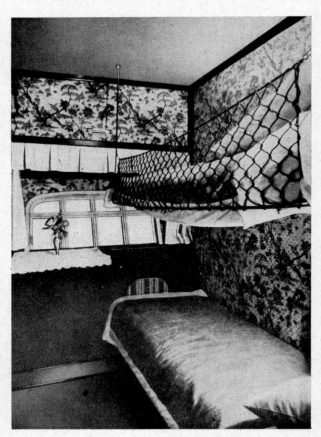

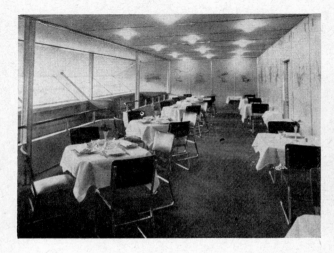

total of 2,650 h.p. and a range of 12,427 miles. Her achievements were greater. Starting in 1929 with an epic round-the-world flight of 21,500 miles in twenty days, the *Graf Zeppelin* went on to pioneer transatlantic air travel, making more than 140 crossings and carrying 13,110 passengers in her eight years of service.

In 1936 she was joined, and finally replaced, by a fine new Zeppelin named the *Hindenburg*, which began a regular non-stop service between Germany and New York. It was not a fast service, the best flying time being about sixty-two hours, but never had such comfort been provided in an aircraft. There was even a lightweight grand piano aboard. Then, on 6th May, 1937, whilst being moored at Lakehurst, New Jersey, the *Hindenburg* suddenly burst into a mass of flames and was destroyed. Following as it did disasters to the British R. 101, French *Dixmude*, American *Shenandoah*, *Akron* and *Macon*, world confidence in the airship seemed to die with the *Hindenburg* and yet another chapter of aviation progress was closed.

Smaller, non-rigid airships are still used by the U.S. Navy for anti-submarine patrol and radar warning duties over the sea, where they are unlikely to encounter enemy aeroplanes. But, by and large, the sleek, graceful airship seems to have given way permanently to the noisy, hurrying aeroplane, in the same way that the beautiful old sailing clippers had to make way for ocean steamers. Progress demands speed, and the airship could never be really fast.

Perhaps surprisingly, the balloon has outlived the airship in its usefulness. Every day, meteorological balloons are released all over the world, to radio back information on the different layers of the atmosphere which they pass through in their silent climb to 100,000 ft. or more. This data plays a vital part in enabling airliners to choose the safest, fastest routes—and it is only a start. Officers and doctors of the U.S. Air Force and Navy have been carried to similar heights, sealed in tiny aluminium gondolas under huge plastic balloons, as part of a research programme to

The magnificent old *Graf Zeppelin*, seen here over its shed at Friedrichshafen, became as famous in peacetime as its predecessors had been in war. After making a superb round-the-world flight in 1929, it went into service as a passenger-carrying airliner. During the next eight years it made more than 140 Atlantic crossings, and carried a total of 13,110 passengers throughout its life.

Major J. W. Kittinger of the United States Air Force inside the tiny aluminium gondola of the balloon which carried him to a height of 96,000 ft. Packed with research instruments, it was his private world for twelve hours. He has made a parachute jump from a similar balloon, from a height of 76,400 ft.

discover if man can survive in space, where there is no atmosphere to shield him from the deadly radiation which bombards the Earth ceaselessly. One of them, Major J. W. Kittinger, has even made a parachute jump from the gondola of this type of balloon at a height of 76,400 ft., to prove that a man can bale out of an aeroplane at such heights and live.

So it cannot be said that the years, and the lives, spent on developing lighter-than-air aircraft were wasted.

*   *   *

Going back now well over a century, to the year 1842, we find that little progress had

been made towards building a powered aeroplane since Sir George Cayley turned his attention from gliders to airships. But in that year a young inventor named Samuel Henson designed a remarkable Aerial Steam Carriage, based on Cayley's theories and his own experiments with model gliders. We know quite a lot about this aircraft, for in 1843 Henson enlisted the help of another enthusiast named John Stringfellow, and together they built a 20-ft. model of the Aerial Steam Carriage which can still be seen in the National Aeronautical Collection at South Kensington.

It looks crude by modern standards, yet its design is more like that of a modern aeroplane than many aircraft which later flew successfully. Unfortunately, before trying to prove that it would fly, Henson let his imagination run riot. He issued pictures of the aircraft in flight over London, France and even the Pyramids, and then tried to get a Bill passed in Parliament to authorise the setting up of an Aerial Steam Transit Company to operate world-wide air services with Steam Carriages. As might be expected, the whole thing was greeted with ridicule by Parliament and the Press, and when his model failed to work in 1847, Henson lost heart and emigrated to America.

Stringfellow decided to carry on the experiments alone, and many aviation historians have recorded that his 10-ft. span model based on the Steam Carriage made the first flight in history by a powered aeroplane in 1848. Unfortunately there seems little evidence to support this claim and the next truly great name after Cayley and Henson is that of Félix Du Temple, a captain in the French Navy. This gentleman, in about 1857, designed and built a little 1½-lb. clockwork-powered aeroplane which took off from the ground, made a genuine free flight and then landed safely.

At this stage, it might be as well to define precisely what is considered to be a true flight. As a start, the aircraft must rise from the ground solely under its own power, sustain itself in the air for a reasonable period under the control of its pilot, and land at a spot no lower than that at which it left the ground. This may seem fairly obvious; but because there has never been any general agreement on what, for example, represents "a reasonable period" or distance covered, there are still persistent and quite ridiculous arguments as to who was first to fly in the world and in the United Kingdom.

In fact, it is of little importance who was first to leave the ground. What really matters is to give honour to all the great pioneers whose courage and genius led to really practical aeroplanes.

Félix Du Temple more than earned his place among them, for he followed up his

Typical imaginative picture of Samuel Henson's proposed Aerial Steam Carriage. A model of it, made by Henson and Stringfellow in 1847, is in the National Aeronautical Collection, South Kensington.

model with a full-size machine on the same lines. Although it looks strange to our modern eyes, it combined most of the good features of Henson's Steam Carriage with a few new ones that gave it more chance of success. We do not know as much about it as we should like, but it seems reasonable to assume that the body was made of aluminium, as Du Temple suggested this in his patent, as a means of saving weight. Certainly the wings were set at a dihedral angle, as suggested by Cayley, to improve stability, and a tractor propeller was used instead of Henson's "pushers".

Piloted by a young sailor, this aeroplane took off down a short inclined ramp at Brest in about 1874 and made a brief hop through the air. Nobody claims that it did more; but no more could be expected when we remember that it was powered by a primitive hot-air engine.

Otto's internal-combustion engine, and Daimler's improved version, were still in the future. In general, this was a blessing in disguise, as it prevented many would-be aviators from killing themselves: but a few of the more skilled designers came near to success even though they were compelled to use heavy steam-engines.

Some Russian writers still claim that I. N. Golubev was the first to fly in A. F. Mozhaisky's steam-driven monoplane, in July 1884. The truth is that it hopped 65–100 ft. after taking off down a ramp, like Du Temple's aeroplane.

Similarly, it has often been claimed that Clément Ader of France was first, since he flew for about 165 ft. in his bat-wing *Eole* at Armainvilliers on 9th October, 1890. A close study of the aircraft shows that it could hardly have satisfied the requirement for *controlled* flight; but this was almost certainly the first take-off by an aeroplane solely under its own power, and was more successful than Ader's later attempt to fly in his twin-engined *Avion III*, in October 1897.

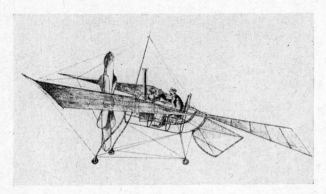

The aeroplane, designed by Félix Du Temple, which made the first-ever powered hops in about 1874 is believed to have looked like this. It became airborne only after running down a slope to gain speed.

A British contender for the honour was Sir Hiram Maxim who, in 1894, built a 4-ton steel-tube aircraft, bigger than a Viscount airliner, not with any idea of flying but purely to test some of his theories. A guard rail was fitted to prevent it rising more than 2 ft. from the ground, but, on the third test, with Maxim and two mechanics aboard, the huge contraption developed so much lift under the impetus of its two 180-h.p. steam engines that it broke free of the guard rail and made a brief "flight" before crashing.

Once again, it is necessary only to look at the aeroplane to see that its pilot could never have controlled it in a real flight; and the biplane tested by Karl Jatho of Germany in the summer and autumn of 1903 appears no more capable of controlled and sustained flight. Thirty years afterwards, Nazi Germany erected a monument to Jatho, as "the first powered-flier in the world", claiming that he flew for 59 ft. on 18th August, 1903, and almost 200 ft. three month's later. Unfortunately, he had no witnesses, because he was a civil servant and believed that any publicity would harm his career. Nor do we know if the ground was flat, or if he took off down a slope. As a result, even German historians do not consider that Jatho deserves the words on his monument.

Why did none of these pioneers succeed? They no longer lacked the power to fly after 1886 and could have learned enough from the writings and experiments of people like Cayley, Henson and Du Temple to build a reasonably-efficient aeroplane. The simple answer is that most of them built an aeroplane to their own ideas and then tried to fly it, instead of finding out first what made an aeroplane fly and then designing a machine to make the best use of this knowledge. In brief, they lacked a scientific approach.

That is why the story of the first successful flight began with a man who never got as far as fitting an engine to his aeroplanes. His name was Otto Lilienthal, and he made no attempt to leave the ground until he had spent years studying everything that had been written about flying and doing research and calculations. Finally, in 1891, he made a beautifully-simple and light bird-like glider of peeled willow wands covered with waxed cotton cloth. This flew so well that he built an artificial hill near Berlin as a jumping-off place for his flights, of which he made more than 2,000 in the next five years.

After each day's gliding, Lilienthal tabulated the results and gradually improved the design of his gliders until he could cover ¼

Another machine which managed to fly briefly after taking off down a slope was Alexander Mozhaisky's big steam-powered monoplane of 1884. The pilot was not Mozhaisky himself, pictured above, but I. N. Golubev.

The giant 4-ton, steam-powered aeroplane built by Sir Hiram Maxim in 1894. It achieved a brief uncontrolled "flight" at Bexley, Kent. Wing span was 104 ft., length 120 ft. and wing area 4,000 sq. ft.

mile at heights up to 75 ft. But he made the fatal mistake of relying on movement of his body in the air to control the glider's flight; and on 9th August, 1896, at the age of forty-eight, he lost control, crashed and died.

What made his loss more tragic was that he was about to build a powered version of his glider, which would almost certainly have flown successfully. Instead, it was left to his "disciples", Percy Pilcher in England and Octave Chanute in America, to carry on where he had ended. Within three years, Pilcher had built a powered version of his highly-successful glider, the *Hawk*; but he too crashed and died before he could test it.

Despite these setbacks, it must have been clear at the turn of the century that the first powered flight was very near. Cayley had

provided the basic theories. Henson had begun to translate them in terms of a complete aeroplane. Du Temple had carried the process one stage further. Francis Wenham had not only built the first wind tunnel for aviation research, but had read a paper on *Aerial Locomotion* before the first meeting of the Aeronautical Society, in 1866, which confirmed many of Cayley's beliefs and laid down almost every basic principle upon which the theory and practice of aviation are founded. Lilienthal had proved beyond any shadow of doubt that human flight in heavier-than-air craft was possible. Otto and Daimler had produced the power for flight. In Australia, Lawrence Hargrave had perfected the box-kite, combining good lifting qualities with sturdy structure. And, in America, Octave

29

Otto Lilienthal, who made thousands of successful flights in monoplane, biplane and multiplane gliders in the 1890s, and so helped to prove the practicability of human flight.

Chanute had written a book entitled *Progress in Flying Machines*, in which he collected together all worthwhile data on aeronautical design up to that time.

Chanute's book and the achievements of Lilienthal made such an impression on the minds of Orville and Wilbur Wright, two young bicycle-makers of Dayton, Ohio, that they decided they had to fly. From the start they had no doubt that they would do so and, like Lilienthal, they went about the job in a scientific manner. Having learnt all they could about the successes and failures of earlier would-be airmen, they knew that the key to success was to achieve stability (or balance)

and control in flight. Finding a suitable engine could come later.

For three years they worked patiently, never taking unnecessary risks. They began in 1900 by building a tail-first biplane glider, which was controlled by means of an elevator at the front and by warping (twisting) the wing-tips—a technique which had the same effect as moving our modern ailerons. This first glider was flown mainly as a kite, at the end of ropes. It worked so well that Orville and Wilbur built a larger and, so they thought, better glider in the following year: but when they first tried to fly it, at Kitty Hawk, in North Carolina, they found its performance disappointing. So they went home, built a primitive wind tunnel from an old starch-box and tested dozens of tiny model wings in it.

It soon became apparent that most of the data that had been published about lift from wings of various sections was inaccurate. So they built a new glider, with wings based on the most efficient of their models and with a rudder at the rear, and made about 1,000 flights in this in the autumn of 1902. The time was now ripe, they felt, to try fitting an engine to a glider of this type: but it looked as if they would be too late to claim the honour of being first to fly.

Seven years earlier, in 1896, Dr. Samuel Pierpont Langley, Secretary of the great Smithsonian Institution, had flown a 16-ft.-span tandem-wing steam-powered model aeroplane well over ½ mile at 25 m.p.h. The U.S. War Department had promptly decided to finance the construction of a full-size aircraft on the same lines and this was now ready for its first flight test.

Langley named his machine the *Aerodrome*, and it was powered by a remarkable five-cylinder radial petrol engine which produced 52 h.p. and weighed only 125 lb. Designer of the engine was Charles Manly, who was both Langley's chief assistant and test pilot. Unfortunately, he was never given a chance to prove his skill, for as the *Aerodrome* was catapulted off a houseboat on the Potomac River on 7th October, 1903, it snagged a post on the launching track and plunged into the water. A second attempt, on 8th December, ended the same way, the wings and tail of the *Aerodrome* being so damaged before it left the catapult that it collapsed and crashed.

Always ready to belittle the pioneers of flying, the press treated the affair as a huge joke. One Boston newspaper commented: "If Professor Langley had only thought to launch his air-ship bottom up, it would have gone into the air instead of down into the water." Dispirited, and with no money for further experiments, Langley gave up, and the coast was clear for the Wright brothers after all.

On 17th December, Orville lay on the lower wing of their powered biplane, which they called the *Flyer*, and put his shoulders in the harness that controlled the wing warping. The 12-h.p. home-made engine was started, and just after 10.35 a.m. the biplane began moving forward along its wooden launching track, with Wilbur running beside it, steadying the wing-tip.

The five men and a boy who made up the audience for one of the most dramatic events in history saw the biplane suddenly lift itself into the air. Desperately, Orville tried to keep it level, but the front elevator was so powerful that this was almost impossible. Even a slight movement caused the *Flyer* to lurch 10 ft. higher, and as soon as he tried to correct this by turning the elevator the aircraft began diving to the ground. Its point of touchdown was 120 ft. from where it left its track—less than the wing-span of many modern airliners. It had been airborne only 12 seconds and nobody would claim that this flight had been properly controlled.

Judged by itself, therefore, this now-accepted first powered flight in history would hardly have qualified for such a title. But it was followed on that same day by three more flights, on the last of which Wilbur flew

Preparing for the first flight test of Professor Langley's aeroplane, which he named the *Aerodrome*, in October 1903. As it was being launched from this houseboat on the Potomac River, it hit a post and crashed into the water.

852 ft. in fifty-nine seconds. What is more, by December 1904 the Wrights had made flights of more than five minutes, including turns, and by October of the following year they could stay up for half an hour.

Looking back now, and without lessening the glory of the Wright brothers' achievement we know that their aeroplane was a dead-end design. This is, however, of minor importance. What is important is that the apparent ease and confidence with which Orville and Wilbur flew acted as a tremendous inspiration for other pioneers. As late as November 1907 nobody in Europe had built a powered aeroplane that could fly for even a minute. Yet when Wilbur brought a much-improved version of his biplane to France in 1908 he flew for more than two hours on one occasion and carried dozens of passengers. Even King Edward VII of Great Britain travelled to the airfield at Pau to watch him fly. Hard-up pioneers like young A. V. Roe considered it worth cycling there just for a few words with the great man.

In view of all this, it might seem surprising that none of the great designers of that era attempted to copy the Wright biplane. One reason is that Orville and Wilbur understandably did all they could to prevent this, although their 1904-5 flights could hardly be termed "secret" as they were carried out in a large open pasture beside a main road. Their major error was in underestimating the capabilities of designers in Europe, for on 10th October, 1906, Wilbur wrote to a friend: "We do not believe there is one chance in a hundred that anyone will have a machine of the least practical usefulness within five years." In fact, by October 1911 aeroplanes had flown the English Channel and Irish Sea, crossed the Alps, carried official air-mail and boxes of cargo, linked the capitals of England and France and—all too significantly—mounted their first guns.

The fact that Wilbur Wright came all the way to Europe for his first demonstration flights in 1908 reflects the fact that France had become by then the centre of world flying.

17th December, 1903. Orville Wright making the first sustained and controlled flight in a powered aeroplane at Kitty Hawk, North Carolina, while his brother Wilbur runs beside the wing-tip.

The little Brazilian, Alberto Santos-Dumont, flying the aircraft on which he won the Archdeacon Cup for the first official flight in Europe. His "14 bis" biplane had a wing-span of about 40 ft., and a 24-h.p. (later 50 h.p.) Antoinette engine. On 12th November, 1906, it flew 220 metres.

Aviators were welcomed and hero-worshipped in France. Elsewhere they were regarded as either candidates for the nearest padded cell or a menace to public safety, which is why English-born Henry Farman, Lord Brabazon and Paris-born Englishman Hubert Latham did their flying on the other side of the Channel, as did men like Santos-Dumont of Brazil and Chavez of Peru.

Just as there are disputes about who flew first in the world, so there are still arguments as to who was first in Europe. Disregarding, for reasons already given, those who preceded the Wrights, the first claimant is Capt. F. Ferber of France, but his flight in a petrol-driven tractor biplane in May 1905 was made "down-hill". Next on the scene was Traian Vuia of Rumania, who flew 39 ft. in a tractor monoplane in France on 6th March, 1906. This was regarded as no more than a hop; and as there were no observers present when J. C. H. Ellehammer of Denmark left the

ground for 138 ft. on the Island of Lindholm on 12th September that year, the credit for making the first flight in Europe goes officially to our old friend the airship-maker, Alberto Santos-Dumont.

The aeroplane he used, named the 14 *bis*, was a tail-first biplane, made up of a large and a small box-kite fixed at each end of a long, slender fuselage. It was completely without future as a design, but it flew 197 ft. on 23rd October, and this is recognised as the first genuine flight in Europe.

On the whole, therefore, none of the aircraft which made much-publicised early flights had any great future, and the same is true of the first in the United Kingdom. Only recently has it been realised that the first man to fly here was a brilliant, modest experimenter named Horatio Phillips. He was the first to appreciate, as a result of wind-tunnel tests, that a thick wing-section, with different curves on the top and bottom

This may look like a cross between some window shutters and a frame for growing runner beans. In fact it is the aeroplane in which Horatio Phillips almost certainly made the first powered flight in England in 1907. Earlier he had discovered that lift was obtained best from a properly curved wing-section and every slat of his "Venetian blind" aeroplane was a properly-shaped miniature wing. The complete machine was 15 ft. long, 20 ft. wide and 10 ft. high and weighed 500 lb., with its 20–22-h.p. engine. It is said to have flown about 500 ft. during tests at Streatham, London.

surfaces, gave more lift than any other. But instead of building just one large curved wing for his aeroplane he mass-produced little ones and mounted them one above the other so that they looked like a Venetian blind. His basic theories were so right that even the inefficiency of such an arrangement could not prevent success and an unpiloted, tethered version of his aeroplane flew 200 ft. at 40-m.p.h. around a circular track at Harrow in 1893.

In 1904 he built a piloted version which did not work. So he built another, with no fewer than four "Venetian blinds" one behind the other and a 22-h.p. engine; and in this he claimed to have flown about 500 ft. in 1907. There is no reason to disbelieve him, and in any case he would have earned his place among the "men who gave us wings" for his work on wing sections alone.

So far we have not encountered anything that could be termed an aeroplane with a future; but this situation was changing rapidly in 1907.

Foremost among European experimenters at this period were the Voisin brothers, whose box-kite biplanes owed much to the early Wright gliders, and Louis Blériot and Robert Esnault-Pelterie who, with a touch of genius, plumped for the tractor monoplane layout from the start. They were all Frenchmen; but it was Henry Farman who proved the capabilities of the Voisin biplane by winning the Deutsch-Archdeacon prize of £2,000 for the first European circular flight of more than a kilometre, on 13th January, 1908—an achievement which marked the start of practical flying in Europe.

There is no space here to tell of all the pioneers who made this era of flying history the most colourful and interesting of all: but three names stand out supreme in Britain.

One was J. W. Dunne, who realised that most accidents to model aeroplanes and full-size gliders up to that time had been due to lack of "balance" in the air, and believed that the best way of achieving "balance", or stability, was by building swept-wing, tailless aeroplanes. Tests with paper models in 1904 appeared to confirm his theory, and were convincing enough to gain him the official support of His Majesty's Balloon Factory at Farnborough.

"Official support" also means official secrecy. Consequently, as soon as Dunne's first full-size aeroplane, the D.1, had been completed, a party of men from the Army Balloon and Kite Section were put into civilian clothes and packed off to the Duke of Atholl's estate in Scotland to test it. The Duke was, by tradition, allowed to maintain a private army, so there was little fear of uninvited observers, and the tests were carried out quickly and satisfactorily. The D.1's two 12-h.p. Buchet engines failed to work properly, but after they had been removed it flew sufficiently well as a glider to justify development of further aircraft on the same lines.

While all this was happening, the Factory's other designer, American-born "Col." S. F. Cody, was also making progress. He was a remarkable character, combining rare skill and courage with a love of showmanship. Like his namesake, Col. "Buffalo Bill" Cody, he had spent several years as a scout in the wild west, hunting "buffalo" and fighting Indians. He was a superb shot, tremendously strong, and always wore a goatee beard and long hair, which usually sprouted from under an enormous stetson hat. Furthermore, he was seen astride a richly saddled white horse almost as often as on the pilot's seat of an aeroplane.

Cody joined the Factory in 1906 as Chief Instructor to the Man-lifting Kite Section. Given a fair wind, its large kites could be used to lift a man in a basket as easily as could a balloon, without inflation problems, and Cody lost no time in fitting a 12-h.p. Buchet engine in one of them and proving that it would fly as an aeroplane, minus pilot.

From there it was but a short step to building a full-size piloted version of the same thing; and on 16th October, 1908, Cody used this aircraft to make the officially-recognised first flight in a piloted aeroplane in Great

Another picture in which things are not quite what they seem to be. The be-whiskered gentleman with the stetson hat and white horse was the former scout and buffalo-hunter S. F. Cody, but the photograph was taken in England not the Wild West. It shows Cody supervising an ascent by one of his man-carrying kites at H.M. Balloon Factory, Farnborough, in 1906. From such kites he developed the aeroplane in which he made the first officially-recognised powered flight in the United Kingdom.

Cody flying his Biplane No. 3, the famous *Cathedral*, over Laffan's Plain, Farnborough, in 1909.

Britain, covering a measured distance of 496 yards at a height of 50–60 ft. over Laffan's Plain, Farnborough.

Six months later the War Office decided to abandon aeroplane experiments, as the cost, which totalled £2,500 by then, was considered too great! By comparison, Germany spent something like £400,000 on military aviation in that same year of 1909.

Fortunately, the Government's decision had little effect on British aeroplane development. Dunne and Cody continued their work privately, and several other designers had entered the picture by that time.

Foremost among them was a young man named Alliott Verdon-Roe, who in 1906 had travelled to the United States on behalf of a Mr. Davidson, the designer of an incredible helicopter with 240 rotor blades. The helicopter never achieved any success; but Roe

did. He started in 1907 by winning first prize at a flying competition for model aeroplanes organised at Alexandra Palace by the *Daily Mail*, and then set about building a man-carrying version of his successful biplane model, in the hope of winning £2,500 offered by the management of Brooklands to the first aviator able to fly round their motor-racing track before the end of 1907.

The importance of such prizes cannot be over-estimated. Few of the pioneers were wealthy, and even though their aeroplanes were usually frail contraptions of stick, wire and canvas, they still cost a lot of money.

Unfortunately, the Brooklands management seem to have offered their prize in a half-hearted manner, for when A. V. Roe asked permission to build his full-size aeroplane there he was hardly greeted with open arms. Having built his workshop in an agreed position near the judges' box, he was first told to move it to a less conspicuous position and paint it dark green, then asked to make it available as an extra refreshment room during motor races. His tests had to be made before anyone arrived with a car, which meant starting work at dawn; yet he was forbidden to sleep in his shed. To get over this problem, he usually said "Good night" to the gate-keeper, walked out and then climbed back over the fence! What is more, he had to live on about 5s. worth of food each week in order to be able to afford the parts for his aeroplane.

Such hardships had their compensations, for on 8th June, 1908, Roe, after taxying his biplane across the track for a short while, suddenly felt the wheels leave the ground and realised that he was flying. Although it was too late to try to win the £2,500 prize, his achievement still gave him a big thrill. He regarded it chiefly as a step forward in a lengthy programme of research, little realising that this short flight would cause one of the biggest controversies in aviation history twenty years later, when a committee of the Royal Aero Club had the unenviable task of deciding who was the first Englishman to

fly in Britain. This honour was finally accorded to J. T. C. Moore-Brabazon (now Lord Brabazon of Tara), who made a flight of nearly 500 yards in his French-built Voisin at the Isle of Sheppey in the spring of the following year. Roe's exploit was considered too short to constitute a proper sustained and controlled flight, while Cody was, of course, American at the time of his earliest flights. The Phillips' flight appears to have been overlooked.

Nevertheless, Roe stands out as one of the greatest British pioneers, and on 13th July, 1909, he made certain of one "first" with what is regarded officially as the first flight in an all-British aeroplane. The little triplane with which he accomplished this is today one of the prized exhibits of the National Aeronautical Collection, and is the more remarkable for the fact that it is covered with brown paper and has an engine of only 9 h.p.

Success did not end his troubles, for, having already been thrown out of Brooklands, he was next asked to leave Lea Marshes, where he built and tested his triplane. The local authorities had, in fact, just decided to take him to court as a danger to the public when

Carrying A. V. Roe's first aeroplane out of its shed on to the race-track at Brooklands in 1908. To avoid possible damage from passing the machine over the spiked railings, Roe made a section of the railings quickly removable, without telling the owners, who had already made the experiments almost impossible with their restrictions. His 1908 flights in this Avroplane are regarded officially as no more than hops, but he went on to become the greatest of our British pioneers.

In July 1909, A. V. Roe made the first officially-recognised flights by an Englishman in a British aeroplane, at Lea Marshes, in this tiny brown-paper-covered triplane. Far from treating him as a hero, the local authorities decided to summon him as a danger to the public. One of the charges was that he kept awake the tramps who slept on the Marshes. The summons was dropped after Louis Blériot flew the Channel.

Louis Blériot managed to keep the engine of one of his aeroplanes going long enough to fly the Channel and so win a *Daily Mail* prize of £1,000. Few people realised the full military significance of the flight, but the authorities at Lea Marshes could hardly charge Roe with the "crime" of wanting to fly, when the same ambition had brought fame to a Frenchman. So the case was dropped.

With A. V. Roe and Louis Blériot added to

(*Continued on page 40*)

J. T. C. Moore-Brabazon prepares to make the first official flight in Britain by a British pilot, in May, 1909. His aeroplane is the French-built Voisin *Bird of Passage*.

25th July, 1909. Louis Blériot at Dover after the first successful Channel flight. His Blériot XI monoplane had a wing span of 25 ft. 6 in. and was powered by a 24-h.p., three-cylinder Anzani engine. He would probably have failed had he not flown through a rain shower, which cooled the engine just as it was beginning to overheat. Even then it would not produce sufficient power to carry him over the white cliffs of the Kent coast. He had to fly along them until he came to a cleft, through which he flew and flopped down heavily on to this meadow near Dover Castle.

The biplanes used for racing in 1909–10 were often flat out at 40 m.p.h., but there was plenty of excitement. Crashes occurred often, but the aircraft were so frail that they crumpled, absorbing much of the shock of impact with the ground. As a result, fatal accidents were surprisingly few in number.

The 1909 Blériot monoplane is of wood construction, both wing and fuselage being wire-braced to impart the necessary strength and rigidity.

The thin, flexible wings carry no ailerons; instead, the complete wing panels are warped or twisted to balance the aircraft in flight.

(1) 24-h.p. three-cylinder "fan type" Anzani engine, air-cooled. (2) Brass fuel tank, cylindrical with doomed ends. (3) Fabric laced to sides and bottom of fuselage. The entire fuselage top, engine bay and aft end of fuselage is left uncovered. (4) Air flotation bag for emergency descent on water. (5) Rudder. (6) Rudder control cable (7) Elevator (shown in an "up" position for climb). This rotates about the ends of fixed tailplane. (8) Fixed tailplane, braced to fuselage with steel struts. (9) Elevator control cable. (10) Castoring tailwheel. (11) Steel spring shock-absorber.

the list of aviation's earlier great pioneers, it might be said that we have come to the end of the story of the "men who gave us wings". From 1909 flying never looked back and progress was rapid—thanks in large measure to the appearance of reliable new engines like the little Gnome rotary, which powered a high proportion of the best aircraft of the next seven years.

With safe and efficient aeroplanes now being built in increasing numbers, it was inevitable that somebody should suggest matching them against one another, and most leading French, British and American airmen competed in the world's first flying meeting at Rheims in August 1909. A quarter of a million people attended, and they got their

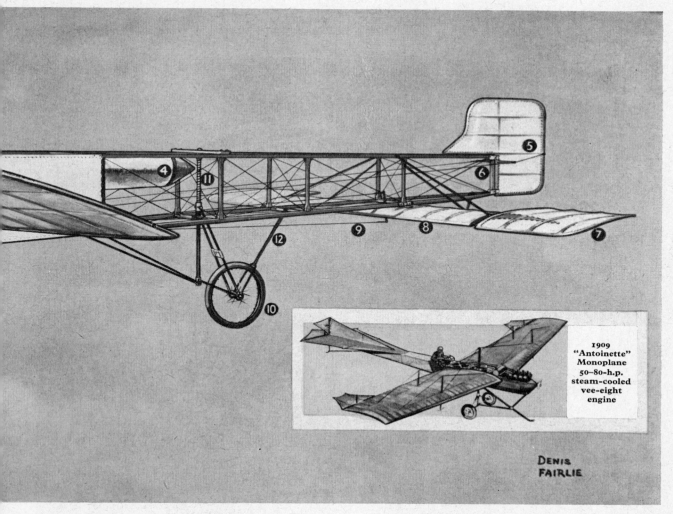

1909
"Antoinette"
Monoplane
50–80-h.p.
steam-cooled
vee-eight
engine

DENIS
FAIRLIE

(12) **Rubber cord to restrain wheel from swinging in flight.** (13) **Main undercarriage struts (wood).** (14) **Steel tube undercarriage strut.** (15) **Sliding collar, attached by cable to** (16) **rubber shock-absorbers.** (17) **Wire-spoked main wheel (pneumatic tyre); moves up and down for springing and free to castor about** (18) **hinge joint.** (19) **Compression strut; receives landing shocks by sliding collar** (15) **up tube** (14) **thereby stretching rubber shock-absorbers.** (20) **Steel tube cabane.** (21) **Steel tube pylon.** (22) **Steel tape flying wires to front spar.** (23) **Landing wires.** (24) **Wing warping wires fixed to** (25) **pulley and rear spar.** (26) **Wing warp wires pass freely over** (27) **pulley fixed to cabane.** (28) **Warp control cable.** (29) **Bell-shaped aluminium member fixed to control column. To warp wings, column is moved to either side; this rotates the lower pulley which, via the cables, pulls down the rear spar of one wing panel and lifts the opposite panel. The wings twist about the front spar, which remains fixed. Compared with today's aircraft, notice the hollow concave rib section of both mainplane and tailplane.**

money's worth of excitement. Records were broken every day, and Glenn Curtiss, the greatest U.S. pioneer after the Wrights, reached the staggering speed of 50 m.p.h. in one event. There were several crashes, but nobody was killed, so they were regarded as all part of the fun and flying meetings began to have their place in the sporting calendar all over the world.

There was no longer any doubt of the aeroplane's success as a sporting machine, and Blériot, Farman and the Voisin brothers were soon turning out aeroplanes at full speed from their modest factories. Other French firms were busy building Wright biplanes; and Blériot opened a flying school. In England, the brothers Horace, Eustace and Oswald

Short, who had been for some years official balloon-makers to the (later Royal) Aero Club, established a factory at Shellbeach to build Wrights; while over in America the U.S. Army bought its first aeroplane—another Wright—and Glenn Curtiss offered *June Bug* biplanes at about £1,000 each. Aviation was fast leaving the "trial and error" stage and becoming an industry, sufficient to justify an Aero Show even at Olympia, where the British public were able to inspect at close quarters no fewer than eleven aeroplanes— including two weird and wonderful "orthopters"—and a whole range of aero-engines. Nor was it any longer a sport only for men, for on 22nd October, 1909, Mme la Baronne de Laroche flew solo for 300 yards in a Voisin at Chalons, and so became the first of many brilliant women pilots.

Nor was flying any longer a mere sport. It was not yet reliable enough to become a

This picture, taken at the world's first flying meeting at Rheims in 1909, shows Sommer and Farman battling around the race-course in their Voisin biplanes. Farman set up world duration and distance records and collected £2,500 in prize money.

means of public transport—except for the Zeppelin service in Germany—but de Lana's

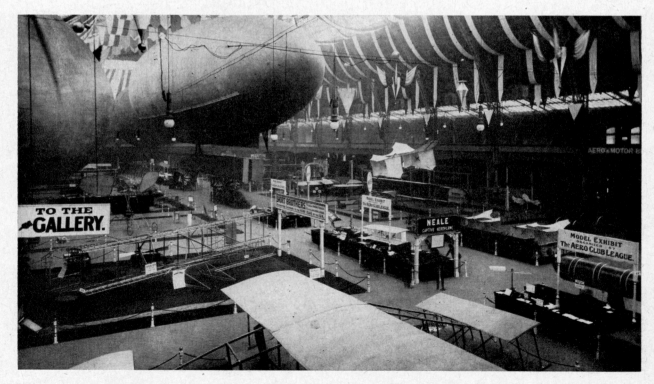

Following the success of the world's first aero exhibition, staged in the Grand Palais in Paris in 1908, a British Aero Show was held at Olympia in March, 1909. All the really practical aeroplanes displayed were French.

Aviation becomes an industry. A corner of the main assembly floor at the British and Colonial (Bristol) factory in 1910.

old fear that aircraft might be used for war began to be justified.

In America, Eugene Ely flew a Curtiss biplane off and on to warships, promising long-range reconnaissance "eyes" for the world's battle-fleets and foreshadowing the aircraft carrier of the future. Aeroplanes began to sprout guns and bombs experimentally. Antoinette in France even built an aeroplane that was armoured against ground fire—although it must be added that it was too heavy to fly more than a few yards. Two Bristol Boxkite biplanes took part in Army manoeuvres on Salisbury Plain in September 1910, during which the first wireless messages were transmitted from an aircraft in flight to a ground station. Within two more years Britain had a properly-established Royal Flying Corps, with Military and Naval Wings.

Most of the aircraft bought for the R.F.C. were French-built which led to a great deal of criticism, especially by the British aircraft industry! They were given a chance to prove the superiority of their own designs in the Military Trials of 1912, which were won convincingly by Cody's *Cathedral*. But it was a most unsuitable aircraft for military use and won mainly because of its mighty 120-h.p engine. It was not until A. V. Roe produced his revolutionary Type 500 tractor biplane,

43

followed in 1913 by T. O. M. Sopwith's superb little Tabloid, that British designs began to lead the world. The Tabloid could fly at 92 m.p.h. on only 80 h.p. and this, combined with a War Office ban on monoplanes following a series of accidents, seemed to establish the superiority of the tractor biplane and retarded monoplane development for something like twenty years.

The R.F.C. had only 63 aeroplanes when war was declared on 4th August, 1914. Many were out of date; all were unarmed. By comparison, Germany had 260 military aircraft and France 156. But the British aircraft industry had proved its ability to turn out world-beating aeroplanes, and the factory at Farnborough, although busy designing and

Britain's counterpart to Eugene Ely was Cdr. C. R. Samson of the Royal Navy, who flew a Short S. 27 biplane off a platform on H.M.S. *Africa* in January 1912. Four months later he achieved a much greater success by flying the same aircraft from H.M.S. *Hibernia* (*above*) while the vessel was steaming at 10½ knots during a review of the fleet by King George V.

Another 1912 exploit in a Short biplane was the first flight through Tower Bridge, London, by Frank McClean on 10th August (*left*). He then hopped and taxied under the remaining bridges to Westminster where he alighted. Reprimanded by the police, he promised not to leave the water again until he had taxied the seaplane downriver, past Tower Bridge. When he did attempt to take off, he crashed.

Igor Sikorsky's giant *Ilia Mourometz*, developed from his *Le Grand*, the world's first four-motor aeroplane. Its cabin was fitted with tables, chairs and couches, and passengers were able to walk on a promenade deck above the fuselage during flight, as shown above. It was powered by four 100-h.p. Argus engines, and went into production as a bomber for the Russian air force in the 1914–18 War.

producing aircraft, was slowly developing into the vast research organisation which, renamed the Royal Aircraft Establishment, has done much to ensure the continuation of British leadership in the air since 1914.

When the First World War started, the military aeroplane was still largely a novelty. The Army had vague ideas about using it for reconnaissance; the Navy thought it would be useful for over-water patrol; but it was not yet a fully fledged fighting machine. Four years later, British military aviation had become such a vital part of our armed forces that it was removed from the control of the older Services and provided with a separate Air Ministry to take care of its welfare.

Tennyson's 19th-century vision of the "nations' airy navies grappling in the central blue" was no longer fiction. Pilots in swift, heavily armed fighter 'planes shot each other out of the sky over the Western Front; reconnaissance 'planes reported and photographed every movement of the unhappy armies on the ground; bombers showered high-explosive and incendiary bombs on battlefield and town alike; the first dive-bombers had been built to harass further the infantryman in his muddy trench; torpedo-planes had scored their first victories against ships at sea; frail seaplanes had, to a large extent, given way to carrier-based fighters and bombers; and big long-range flying-boats had helped to check the menace of the U-boats round these islands.

The aircraft industry of Britain alone had grown from small scattered factories, peopled with a few visionaries and craftsmen, to a vast complex industry, employing 350,000 men and women, and producing aeroplanes at the rate of nearly 30,000 a year—all for war. Little wonder that Orville Wright commented sadly: "What a dream it was; what a nightmare it has become."

Famous Aircraft
of 1914–1918

The two pictures above show line-ups of aircraft flown by the greatest British and German fighter aces of the 1914–18 War. On the left are S.E. 5A's of No. 85 Squadron of the R.A.F. at St. Omer, France on 21st June, 1918. On the right are brightly-coloured Albatros scouts belonging to the famous Richthofen "circus". Below them (*centre right*) is one of the first heavy night bombers, a Handley Page 0/400, under tow with its wings folded.

Most formidable fighter of the 1914–18 War was the Sopwith Camel, destroyer of 1,281 enemy aircraft in combat.

Still flying in America is this reconstructed Spad VII, as flown by the top U.S. ace, Eddie Rickenbacker.

The two-seat Bristol Fighter (*top left*) was not only a match for German single-seaters but remained in service with the R.A.F. long after the 1914–18 War had ended. Another great British aircraft was the D.H. 4 day bomber (*left*), the finest machine of its type in the world and capable of outpacing most enemy fighters.

From the enemy camp came the little Fokker Triplane (*top right*). The example illustrated is painted in the blood-red colour scheme adopted by Germany's ace of aces, Manfred von Richthofen, whose favourite mount it was.

This great four-motor bomber was one of the Sikorsky *Ilia Mourometz* aircraft which served with Russia's Squadron of Flying Ships. Seventy were built and they made 400 successful raids for the loss of only one of their number in action.

Behind the scenes at London Airport

A MODERN airport is like a miniature city, with its own shops, restaurants, post offices, bus services, police force, hospital and fire brigade. As well as the airline operators, there are Customs, Health and Immigration officials, petrol companies, cable companies and catering companies. To ensure safe and swift air journeys there are Air Traffic Control, Telecommunications and Meteorological Officers.

Britain's main air terminal is London Airport, some 13 miles to the south-west of London, and not far from Hounslow in Middlesex.

When the R.A.F. required a large transport base near London in 1943, it was realised that the capital would need a new civil airport when peace returned, and consideration was given to this when the present site was chosen.

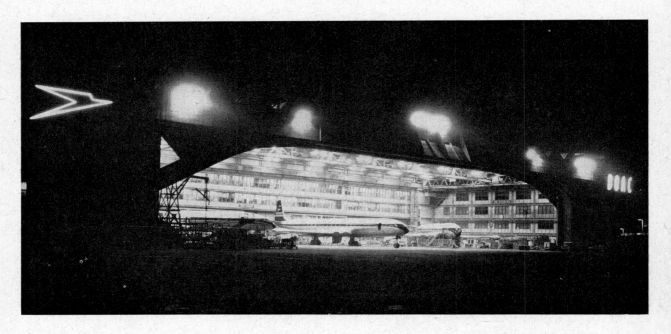

Construction started in May 1944 and followed the R.A.F.'s usual pattern of three runways arranged in a triangle. But the war ended before its completion, and it was handed over to the civil authorities for

Right. **Rising some 127 ft. from the ground the Control Tower dominates the central area and gives the control officers a clear view of the sky in all directions and of all the runways. The distinctive angular shape of the tower minimises the interference which the large flat surfaces of a rectangular building would cause to radio and radar equipment.**

The tower is the nerve centre of the airport. Aerodrome Control—in the circular penthouse on top—regulates movement along the runways and taxiways. Immediately below, Approach Control—readily identified by its large balcony of outward sloping windows—looks after aircraft approaching or leaving the airport.

Below left. **Aerodrome Control Room. A special radar enables the Controller to "see" the runways even in thick fog. A mimic display shows by means of miniature lamps which lights are in use on the airfield itself.**

Below right. **Approach Traffic Control Room. Because they are beyond the range of normal vision, operators in this room rely mainly on radar to "see" the movement of airliners. Their task is to maintain the flow of approaching aircraft in an orderly and safe sequence towards the runway in use.**

immediate development as the main London air terminal. On the R.A.F.'s original triangular layout a second triangle of three runways was superimposed, forming a huge "Star of David" pattern. The advantage of such an arrangement is that two airliners can land and take-off into the wind simultaneously on separate runways.

Even before the runways were completed operations began from the new airport: on

(*Continued on page 55*)

As in the case of other big air terminals, the number of airliners to and from London Airport is now so great that they have to comply with a strict "Highway Code" of the air. Instead of the familiar road signs, traffic lights and policemen on point duty, however, the traffic control system of the air uses a pattern of "air lanes" along which the airliners are guided by radio and radar. Airliners flying to London Airport are directed along specific air lanes until they reach a point where they are handed over to London Airport Approach Control. There are two such "hand-over" points, one near Epsom and one near Watford, and they are "signposted" by radio aids.

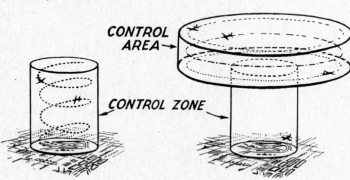

Control Zone—This can best be pictured as a gigantic imaginary "gasometer" of air, several miles in diameter and 1,500 ft. high, covering one or more aerodromes. It is the area in which aircraft make their final landing circuits and approach. No aircraft can enter it without permission, and once there it is under strict radar control to avoid danger of collision.

Control Area—This is a much bigger volume of air, which spreads outwards and upwards to 11,000 ft. on top of a control zone, the two forming a giant mushroom-shaped area. Aircraft approaching to land can be kept circling inside the Control Area at different heights while waiting their turn to descend into the Control Zone landing circuit.

Here we see the Control Area and Control Zone "mushrooms" at three major airports, linked by a system of other Control Areas in the form of "sky-tunnels". All aircraft flying down these tunnels are watched and guided by radar, and the possibility of collision is eliminated by making each one fly at a different height, as shown in the drawing below.

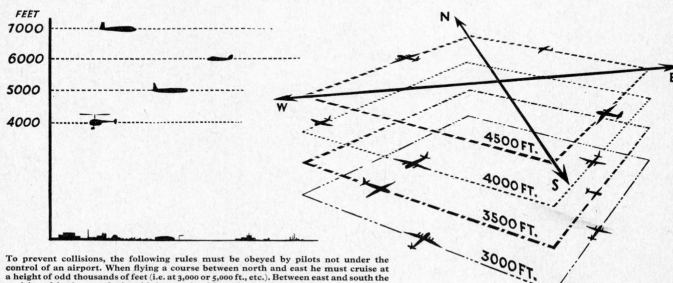

To prevent collisions, the following rules must be obeyed by pilots not under the control of an airport. When flying a course between north and east he must cruise at a height of odd thousands of feet (i.e. at 3,000 or 5,000 ft., etc.). Between east and south the cruising altitude must be in odd thousands of feet plus 500 ft. (i.e. 3,500, 5,500 ft., etc.). from south to west, the height must be in even thousands of ft. (i.e. 4,000, 6,000 ft., etc.). and between west and north the height must be even thousands of feet plus 500 ft. (i.e. 4,500, 6,500 ft., etc.). As can be seen in the diagrams above, this simple method ensures that aircraft flying in opposite directions will be separated by at least 1,000 ft. and can thus never collide.

Queen's Building. This fine building houses airline operations staffs and amenities for visitors who wish to watch the flying; these include a terraced roof garden, an exhibition hall, a news cinema, children's playroom, post office, and a grill room and buffet.

Above. **The cross-bars of the Calvert lighting system provide the pilot with an artificial horizon, helping him to keep his aircraft level as he approaches the runway at night.**

Below right. **The busy scene in the B.O.A.C. Export Freight shed.**

Left. **This furry freight on the hat of B.O.A.C. receptionist Gloria Moyse was one of a £12,000 consignment of chinchillas flown into London Airport.**

Above. **Three of B.O.A.C.'s fleet of Comet 4 jet-liners in the hangar.**

Top right. **A rebuilt propeller is checked for balance on a test rig in the propeller shop.**

Right. **Preparing to hoist a Rolls-Royce Avon turbojet into the wing of a Comet 4.**

Below. **London Airport is the home of the two great British Corporations—B.E.A. and B.O.A.C. Their vast maintenance bases are among the most modern of their kind in the world. The B.O.A.C. Headquarters, 870 ft. long by 432 ft. wide, houses 4,500 people—nearly a quarter of the Corporation's worldwide total.**

Not far from the B.O.A.C. Headquarters is the big B.E.A. Engineering Base. This comprises two large hangars each measuring 900 ft. by 110 ft., or longer than two football pitches, backing on to two workshops. The picture above shows maintenance work in progress on Viscounts in one of the hangars.

Away from the Engineering Base, in LAP Central, B.E.A. prepare food trays in this well-equipped Flight Kitchen.

Close-up of one of the appetising meals prepared in the Flight Kitchen.

Aerial view of the great B.E.A. Engineering Base. To the right centre is the new extension erected to cater for the fleets of Vickers Vanguards and de Havilland Comet 4Bs and 121s which are coming into service in the early 1960's.

General view of London Airport Central. In the centre of the picture is the control tower, with the bow-fronted Queen's Building and passenger-handling terminal behind it. At the top is the B.E.A. Engineering Base.

1st January, 1946, a Lancastrian of British South American Airways, now incorporated with B.O.A.C., took-off on a long distance proving flight to South America.

From this modest beginning has grown the giant air traffic centre we know today, used by more than 40 companies from over 35 different countries.

Catering for 4,000,000 passengers, 130,000 aircraft and 70,000 tons of freight handled each year requires the full time services of nearly 27,000 people.

Only a few of these are ever seen by the ordinary passenger or sightseer, but in this book we have been able to take you behind the scenes.

One Hundred Million Passengers

"HELLO, ladies and gentlemen. Welcome on board the European Airways Stratomaster *Golden Hind*. We shall be taking off for New York in approximately five minutes, and shall cruise at 2,000-m.p.h. at a height of 75,000 ft. Flying time will be 112 minutes. Will you please fasten your seat-belts."

The Sud-Aviation *Caravelle* jet-liner: (1) Weather and anti-collision nose radar. (2) Captain and co-pilot. (3) Radio racks. (4) Forward pantry. (5) Forward entrance door. (6) Forward part of passenger cabin, seating 80 at five abreast. (7) Control runs. (8) Forward-retracting nosewheels. (9) Forward under-floor freight-hold. (10) Emergency exit windows. (11) Main wing-spar attachments. (12) Pressure refuelling valves. (13) Wing fuel tanks, holding 4,100 gallons in all. (14) Port slotted flaps, down for take-off. (15) Port main undercarriage, retracts inward. (16) Rear of passenger cabin. (17) Cloakroom and toilets. (18) Starboard air-brake. Dotted line shows position when raised for landing. (19) Starboard aileron. (20) Starboard slotted flaps, down for take-off. (21) Starboard Rolls-Royce Avon 522 jet engine. (22) Port Rolls-Royce Avon 522 jet engine. (23) Jet exhaust. (24) Hot air de-icing pipe. (25) Hold for hand-luggage, etc. (26) Intake for cabin air-conditioning. (27) Tailplane and fin de-icing pipes. (28) Air-conditioning heat exchanger. (29) Tunnel for stowage of rear passenger-stairway. (30) Elevator and rudder control cables. (31) Rudder power control. (32) Rudder. (33) Port elevator. (34) Position of passenger-stairway when lowered.

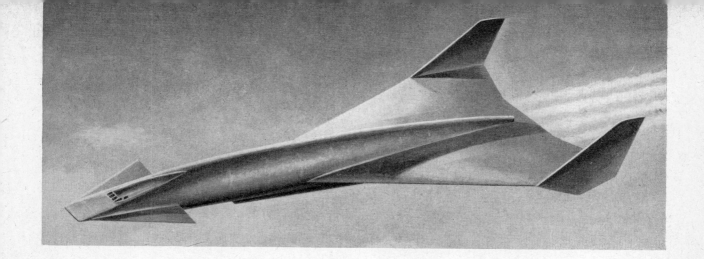

IF the aviation experts are right, that is the kind of message that we shall hear over the public address system of transatlantic airliners by the end of the 1960's. It seems a little hard to believe. After all, with New York time five hours behind London time, it means that we shall land three hours before we take off. If we have just had dinner in London, we

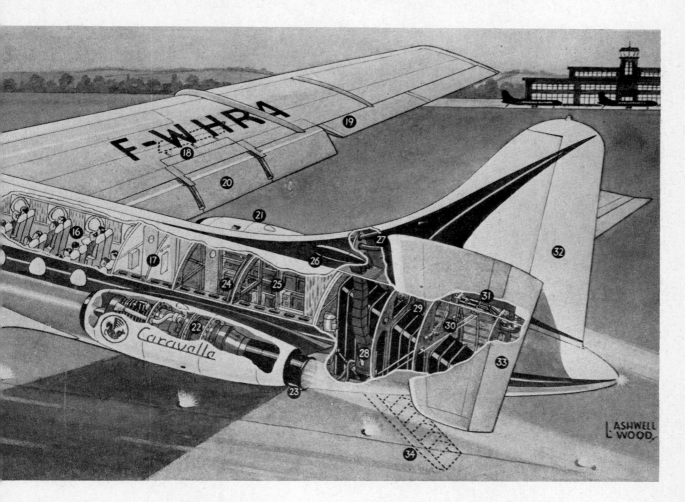

shall find another one waiting for us in America only two hours later—all right for Billy Bunter perhaps, but we do not all have his capacity for food.

We could be in for other surprises too. At least one designer has admitted that it will be best to have no cabin windows in a supersonic airliner, because the cabin will have to be pumped full of air at such a high pressure, to enable the passengers to breathe comfortably at 75,000 ft., that too many cut-outs for windows and doors would weaken the structure. It might also have tilting seats, so that passengers will remain upright even while the airliner is climbing steeply in order to reach its cruising height as quickly as possible.

Is the idea of flying to New York in under two hours beginning to lose some of its appeal? Was flying better in the "good old days" when 'planes were 'planes and pilots really flew them instead of leaving the job to automatic pilots and radar? If you think so, let us go back in imagination to 1920 and see what it was really like.

As a start there was no question of flying very far, because the regular air services were restricted to routes like London to Paris. Even then there was no guarantee that the flight would be non-stop. One aircraft was plagued with engine trouble to such an extent that it had to make twenty-two forced landings *en route* (fortunately not during the Channel crossing) and finally delivered its passengers in Paris two days late.

Of course, it was fun—provided you had an unusual sense of humour and a strong constitution. You were not packed with a hundred other people into a large air-conditioned cabin. In fact there was sometimes no cabin at all and you sat in an open cockpit, because most of the airliners of 1919–20 were converted D.H. 4 or D.H. 9 day-bombers, with passengers instead of an observer and machine-gun to the rear of the pilot. When there was a cabin, it contained two or three

wicker seats into which passengers were crammed face to face, with a lid over their heads. The draughts that came through cracks between the windows and their frames could have been called air-conditioning; but there was no heating. Instead each passenger could borrow a leather flying coat, gloves, helmet and even a hot-water bottle free of charge, as part of the service. It was wonderful. On some over-water routes the airlines even provided parachutes and life-jackets.

The pilot's job was easier too. No maze of knobs, dials and switches confronted him as in a modern airliner. There were few instruments in the open cockpit and even these were hardly worth looking at. For example, there were so many metal parts in the aircraft and the compass was so near the engine that it was often better if the pilot did not trust it. There was no wireless to worry about either, and the only messages which told of an aircraft's progress were reports from places it passed over during its journey.

Navigation was simple. The pilot simply looked over the edge of his cockpit to search for landmarks, and experienced difficulty only when bad weather obscured the familiar straight length of railway line, or the farmhouse where the washing was always hung out at fixed times or the long pier of Calais harbour. Unfortunately, that railway line gave rise to a special problem, for on one occasion when an airliner encountered strong headwinds a train passed it and passengers complained that rail transport was faster than flying. After that pilots had to fly directly over the line, instead of to one side, so that passengers could not see the trains below.

Despite everything, these pioneer air services had a fairly good safety record. There was no night flying and take-off was postponed if the weather looked bad. A forced landing was seldom serious, because the aircraft could get into any reasonably-sized field. One of the few fatal accidents occurred because two pilots were so intent on following a straight

As it was in the beginning. Passengers wrap up warmly before boarding a D.H. 9 airliner of Aircraft Transport and Travel Ltd. for a cross-Channel flight from Croydon in 1920. This particular machine had open cockpits. Most had a primitive enclosed cabin, with wicker chairs and a hinged lid containing windows. Hot-water bottles were provided to keep passengers warm on very cold days.

road whilst flying at the same height in opposite directions that they collided head-on.

When we consider that passenger flying has progressed from such modest beginnings to its present 600-m.p.h. luxury and safety in a mere forty years it becomes easier to believe in that 2,000-m.p.h. Atlantic crossing of 1970. Many problems remain to be solved, but no

The first aeroplane to fly the Atlantic, in easy stages via the Azores, is shown taxying at Lisbon before completing its trip to Plymouth. It was the Curtiss NC-4 flying-boat of the U.S. Navy.

more than have already been overcome by the airlines since 1919.

There were no proper air routes for them to follow then, and an airline can never say simply: "Tomorrow we are going to open a new service from here to Timbuctoo." Each route had to be surveyed, airfields levelled and stocked with fuel and supplies, and essential passenger services provided. That is why the ten years after the end of the 1914–18 War witnessed so many great flights.

The first long-distance route to be conquered was, surprisingly, the most difficult one of all—the North Atlantic. First across, in May 1919, was the big four-engined Curtiss NC-4 flying-boat of the U.S. Navy. It was the only one of three boats which left Newfoundland to complete the trip, via the Azores, and took eleven days. A month later its achievement was overshadowed completely by the first non-stop flight from Newfoundland to Ireland by Captain John Alcock and Lt. A. Whitten Brown, in a converted Vickers Vimy bomber, powered by two Rolls-Royce Eagle engines. Even now, when hundreds of people fly the Atlantic every day with about as much fuss as if they were

14th June, 1919. The Vimy of Alcock and Brown leaving Newfoundland at the start of the first non-stop Atlantic crossing.

bad weather in a machine of wood and canvas and with half the engine-power of a Spitfire. Their subsequent knighthoods and *Daily Mail* prize of £10,000 were richly earned.

Other magnificent flights followed. Two young Australians, Ross and Keith Smith, linked Britain by air with her farthermost Dominions for the first time by flying to Australia in another Vimy. Two Portuguese Naval officers made the first crossing of the South Atlantic in a Fairey seaplane in 1922, and two years later American Air Service pilots completed the first round-the-world flight of 27,534 miles in two Douglas World Cruisers. Another American, Charles Lindbergh, became a world hero overnight in May 1927 by flying alone all the way from New York to Paris in a small Ryan monoplane with a 220-h.p. engine.

catching the 8.22 train to Town, it is not difficult to appreciate the courage of these two Englishmen who flew 1,890 miles through

Douglas World Cruisers of the U.S. Army Air Service made history on 28th September, 1924, when they completed the first successful round-the-world flight. They covered 27,534 miles over 28 countries in an elapsed time of 175 days.

Lindbergh's little 220-h.p. Ryan monoplane, *Spirit of St. Louis*, in which he won world fame on 20th–21st May, 1927, by flying alone 3,600 miles non-stop from New York to Paris in 33½ hours.

All these were great flights and they did much to build up public interest and confidence in aviation. But far more valuable to the development of civil flying was the series of remarkable long-distance flights made in the 1920's by Sir Alan Cobham. He began in 1921, with a 5,000-mile flight round Europe, and gradually became more ambitious until, in 1925–6, he flew from London to Cape Town and back and to Australia and back in a D.H. 50. Then, in 1927, he flew 23,000 miles round Africa in a Short Singapore flying-boat. Following in his footsteps came the great Australian, Sir Charles Kingsford Smith, who in 1928 completed the global network of British pioneering by making a 7,000-mile flight across the Pacific, from California to Brisbane, in the trimotor Fokker *Southern Cross*, and then linked Australia and New Zealand by air for the first time, across the storm-swept 1,400-mile Tasman Sea.

Most of these were proper, planned survey flights, which laid the groundwork for our Empire Air Routes across the world. By the time they were completed, Britain had an airline capable of commercialising at least some of the routes; for on 1st April, 1924, the Government came to the rescue of civil

By the late 1920's, passengers were able to have light meals in flight. On National Air Transport's Ford Trimotors, these consisted of sandwiches in waxed paper and the hot drinks here being handed out.

61

The airliners which, more than any others, made air travel safe, comfortable and popular. Two of Imperial Airways' superb Handley Page Hannibals in front of the control tower at Croydon Airport in the 1930's.

aviation by combining four of our gallant but "hard-up" private companies into a single officially-backed airline named Imperial Air-

The first airline stewardesses were these eight young nurses hired by Boeing Air Transport (later United Air Lines) on 15th May, 1930, to take care of passengers aboard aircraft on its San Francisco–Chicago route.

ways. It was based at Croydon Airport, which had been opened as the air terminal for London in March 1920.

The changeover was a godsend to the aircraft industry, for the new airline soon got down to business, expanding its routes to every corner of the Empire—and it needed a constant succession of newer, better and bigger airliners to meet the competition of such excellent foreign lines as the Dutch K.L.M. company, Swissair, Air France, the Belgian Sabena and German Lufthansa companies. British airliners developed from the small two-passenger, converted de Havilland bombers which carried the first fare-paying passengers from London to Paris in August 1919, to such superb machines as the Handley Page Hannibals, and, in 1936, the famous fleet of Short Empire flying-boats, which introduced new standards of safety, reliability and comfort to world airline travel.

These Empire boats were of particular

Canopus, first of Imperial Airways' great fleet of Short "C" class Empire flying-boats, which made British airline travel second to none for comfort and reliability before World War II.

interest. They marked the change-over to all-metal monoplanes on British civil air routes, and they could go almost anywhere because three-quarters of the world's surface is covered with water, whereas a landplane needed properly laid-out aerodromes from

(*Continued on page 66*)

The gradual increase in airliner size and speed over the past 25 years is well shown in this picture. On the left is a 21-passenger 190-m.p.h. Douglas DC-3 of 1936. To the rear are a DC-4, DC-6 and DC-7. In the foreground is a 176-seat, 600-m.p.h. DC-8 jet-liner.

Some Airliners of Today

Flagship of many of the world's major airlines is the big four-jet Boeing 707 (*top*), which has made possible $6\frac{1}{2}$-hr. transatlantic services from New York to London. Equally-spectacular time saving on shorter routes is offered by the superb French Caravelle jet-liner (*left*) which set a new fashion by carrying its two Rolls-Royce Avon engines on the sides of its rear fuselage. Below it is a Russian Ilyushin Il-18, powered by four 4,015-h.p. Kuznetsov turboprops. Together with the Tupolev Tu-104 twin-jet airliner (*bottom right*) it has been seen often at London Airport in the colours of Aeroflot, the Soviet national airline, and other east European operators.

At the top of the opposite page is a Vickers Viscount, first turboprop airliner to enter service and the most successful British passenger aircraft ever built. Well over 400 have been sold all over the world and experience gained with them has now been built into the larger, faster Vanguard (*centre right*). Although the 425-m.p.h. Vanguard is not so fast as the jets, its four 5,000-h.p. Rolls-Royce Tyne turboprops offer unrivalled economy and it could make possible a £6 London–Paris fare for its 139 passengers.

The twelve-seat club lounge of this Convair 880 jet-liner provides a sharp contrast with the interior of the 1929 Ford Tri-motor illustrated on page 61. The lounge takes up the same space as twelve normal seats.

The veteran Douglas DC-3 is still flying in greater numbers than any other airliner. One reason is that it is ideal for cheap-fare coach-air and inclusive tour services. Another is its splendid reputation for reliability and safety.

which to operate. In practice, it was not quite so simple as this. Sometimes the water was too rough for the flying-boats to land or take off in safety, and there were a number of special hazards connected with water-flying. Pilots sometimes found it hard to judge their height above a smooth sea when landing and flew smack into the water at fairly high speed. Then there was the ever-present danger from floating or water-logged debris, which could hole the boat's thin hull.

Nevertheless, the Empire boats put in wonderful service, enabling Imperial Airways to extend their routes right through to Australia and South Africa, carrying all letters to Empire addresses by air for only 1½d. per ½ oz. (compared with 1s. 6d. to Australia today) and pioneering the first airline services across the North Atlantic in parallel with Boeing Clipper flying-boats of Pan American Airways. It seemed that the big flying-boat was here to stay, for passengers loved its spacious comfort and the feeling of cruising like an ocean liner, at aircraft speeds.

When the first Douglas DC-3 Dakota twin-engined landplane airliner flew in

America in 1936, it seemed likely that this would prove every bit as popular and revolutionary on medium-range routes. Nobody could have foreseen then that the DC-3 would still outnumber any other type in airline service nearly a quarter of a century later—or that by then there would hardly be one flying-boat in regular use on world air routes.

Both of these developments are the direct result of the Second World War which broke out on 3rd September, 1939. The DC-3 was so precisely the right size for use as a standard Allied transport aircraft for troops and supplies that 10,123 were produced for this purpose, to which must be added 803 built in America as civil airliners and many hundreds produced in Russia. Within a year of the war's end, the U.S. Air Force had sold nearly 4,000 of its military models to airlines and many of these are still in service today. Most amazing of all, perhaps, is that one of the original pre-war DC-3s, still flying some 7½ hours a day with North Central Airlines, had amassed the incredible total of 70,817 hours in the air by mid-February 1960, equivalent to nearly 10,300,000 miles of flying.

During its lifetime it has seen the whole pattern of air transport changed. In 1939 the flying-boat was supreme and the aerodromes on which the DC-3 landed were no more than large, flat grass fields. To meet the demands of war huge bomber bases, with concrete runways, were laid down everywhere throughout the world. When the fighting was over, these bases became available for civil flying. So did big landplane airliners like the Douglas DC-4 and Lockheed Constellation which had been developed and put into production as military transports and could therefore be offered for sale at comparatively low prices.

This combination of big, cheap, high-performance landplanes and concrete runways from which to operate them killed the flying-boat.

B.O.A.C. (the successor to Imperial Airways) continued to operate boats for a few years, but the landplanes were faster, just as safe and cheaper to run, because the flying-boat bases had to be maintained and paid for by B.O.A.C. alone, whereas land airports can be used by anyone on payment of just a landing fee.

World's largest airliner is the Russian Tupolev Tu-114, which spans 177 ft., weighs about 180 tons and carries up to 220 passengers. Normal seating is for 170 passengers on routes up to 6,000 miles long, and the four huge 10,000-h.p. Kuznetsov turboprop engines enable the aircraft to cruise at 440–540 m.p.h. The restaurant cabin (*left*) is occupied only during meals, which are supplied from two roomy galleys (*right*) and below-deck kitchens.

This put Britain at a great disadvantage compared with America, because it had been decided during the war that U.S. companies would build all the transport aircraft needed by the Allied air forces, leaving the British aircraft industry free to concentrate on fighters, bombers and other warplanes. As a result, when the war ended, B.O.A.C., B.E.A. and Britain's independent airlines had the choice of making do with aircraft like the Viking and York, which were developed from the Wellington and Lancaster bombers, or of buying machines from America. Work was started on a number of "interim" airliners, designed to fill the gap until the industry could produce a completely new generation of modern aircraft; but these makeshifts were not particularly successful and by the late 1940's it began to look as if Britain would never again be able to compete with America as a manufacturer of airliners.

When the new British airliners did eventually take the air they changed the picture completely. Instead of trying to catch up America's lead in piston-engined aircraft, their designers had taken the bold step of cashing in on our leadership in jet-engine development. First to fly, on 16th July, 1948,

was the medium-range Vickers Viscount, powered by four Rolls-Royce Dart turbo-props and able to cruise at over 300 m.p.h. Then, on 27th July, 1949, came the Comet, first jet airliner in the world, with a cruising speed of about 500 m.p.h.

Some so-called experts saw no future for such machines, claiming that speed was achieved only at the expense of high operating costs and that the jet and turboprop airliners would never pay. What these people forgot was that speed is almost the only advantage air travel has to offer compared with surface travel. As a result, the faster the aircraft flies the more significant this advantage becomes. Nor were the Viscount and Comet merely faster than all other airliners in their class. They were far more comfortable, because the absence of pounding pistons in their engines eliminated the vibration that leads to travel-weariness, and they cruised much higher than other aircraft, above most of the bad weather. What is more, it has since become clear that, operated properly, turbine-powered airliners can be cheaper to run than the piston-engined kind.

The best possible tribute that can be paid to the Comet and Viscount is that soon almost

A Boeing 707 jet-liner is brought in to a perfect landing by the Bell automatic all-weather landing system in right foreground. In bad weather such a system can pick up aircraft 4 miles from the runway and control them through their autopilot all the way to touch-down.

all major airline services will be flown by jet and turboprop aircraft, and this is the second post-war revolution in air travel, following on the switch from flying-boats to landplanes. The third revolution has been the introduction of cheap-fare services.

Until the war, and for a time afterwards, all air fares were first class. When bigger, faster and more economical aircraft began to enter service, ordinary men and women looked forward to the time when they would be able to travel by air at prices they could afford. But fares remained high and, instead of lowering them, airlines began trying to excel each other in the standard of luxury offered to passengers. The limit was reached with services like Pan American's *President* between New York and London, where passengers who could afford a few extra dollars were given red carpet to walk on between the Customs hall and the Strato-cruiser airliner, free orchids for the ladies and cigars for the gentlemen, five-course meals with several different wines and liqueurs, small zip-fastened bags in which to put odds and ends needed during the journey, and so on.

It was all very nice and very popular, but it became more and more apparent that most people who could afford such luxury and who wanted to fly were doing so, and that if airlines wanted to expand their business, the only way was to attract people with less money, even if they had to crowd a few more passengers on each 'plane and cut out free meals to do it. Unfortunately, big airlines cannot cut their fares overnight, for all international fare rates are fixed by the International Air Transport Association, of which most major airlines are members, to avoid undercutting and "price wars" that would bring financial ruin on competitive routes.

So it was not until September 1948 that Pan American were able to open the first regular tourist class service between New York and Puerto Rica. There was no doubt of

Nobody has demonstrated the value of small business aircraft better than Prince Philip, who often travels to official functions in a D.H. Heron of The Queen's Flight. Other royal pilots include King Hussein of Jordan, Prince Bernhard and the Shah of Persia.

its success. Within a year three times as many passengers as before were being carried over the route, without any adverse effect on first class services, which also showed steady improvement, proving that nearly all tourist passengers were people who would not normally have travelled by air. Many were "first-flighters" who, having overcome their fear of flying, became confirmed air travellers.

Within four years tourist class fares were available almost everywhere, even over the Atlantic, and the effect on traffic figures was startling. In the year before their introduction a total of 372,346 people flew the Atlantic, which was less than half the number who went by sea. Within one year the air passengers had increased to 497,021. Within three years the total was 893,072 and they outnumbered for the first time those carried by ship. In 1959, transatlantic air passengers numbered well over 1½ million, of whom 21·5% travelled first class, 4·7% tourist class and a record 73·8% by the still-cheaper economy class. Since then the tourist class has been abandoned and we have the choice of two fares, the difference being in the standard of comfort and service provided, because most aircraft are equipped to carry a proportion of each class.

What has happened on this one route has been duplicated everywhere, and today well over 100 million people fly each year on regular airline services. If we add those who fly in Russia and China, whose airlines issue no figures, and those who go on charter flights as opposed to those on scheduled services, the total is much more than 110 million. To carry them, an airliner has to take off from one of the world's 3,500 airports every four seconds of the day and night, every day of every week of the year. When it is airborne it is never alone, but is in constant radio contact with the ground and other aircraft, and is often being watched and tracked continuously by radar. If it arrives at its destination in bad weather it can be guided to a safe touch-down by radio and radar, and this is only a start. By the mid-60's, the British Autoland system will be able to make the entire landing automatic, without the pilot needing to touch the controls at any stage.

All of this is very wonderful, but there is another side to the picture. The airliners of 1920 could take off from any decent-sized field. Those of 1940 could fly from quite small grass aerodromes. But the big four-jet Boeing 707 and Douglas DC-8 airliners of 1960 must have 2-mile concrete runways from which to operate safely with a full load. Such runways can seldom be provided close to city centres and, in any case, the jet-liners make so much noise that they could not be tolerated if they had to fly low over densely-populated areas. There is the safety aspect to consider too, for most aircraft accidents occur during landing and take-off, and the longer and faster the landing and take-off runs are the greater is the hazard.

So, while the 707 and DC-8 have brought still higher standards of comfort and speed to the airways, linking New York with London in $6\frac{1}{2}$ hours and girdling the Earth in 80

hours, they have also brought immense problems. If we go a stage further and build supersonic airliners without doing something to keep their take-off and landing runs within reasonable limits, there will be even worse problems ahead.

As a result, this is a fitting time to consider whether all our supposed aviation progress has really been progress at all. Forty years ago, aviation promised to bring fast travel to people everywhere. Today the fastest airliners are so big that they can operate only into a small proportion of the world's airports with a worthwhile load. People from outlying areas have to travel long distances to the main international airports before they can emplane, and this wastes a lot of the time that the big jets save.

There are several possible answers to this problem. One is to reduce to a minimum the time lost, by operating a network of feeder services into major airports from the surrounding districts, using the fastest possible aircraft. This is where machines like the turbo-prop Viscount and Friendship score, for they cruise at quite high speeds and can use any airport worthy of the name. For even greater convenience, many large industrial firms have their own private aircraft to carry busy executives on such feeder journeys and on all comparatively short air trips, the aircraft used ranging from four-seat lightplanes like the Piper Tri-Pacer to lavishly-furnished Viscounts, some of them complete with beds and equipment which enables them to be used as mobile hotel room/offices.

However, it seems certain that designers must eventually find ways of shortening the landing and take-off runs of their aircraft. High-lift devices such as wing leading-edge and trailing-edge flaps, and "super-circulation" systems which draw off air from the jet-engines and blow it over the flaps to increase their lift, will all help. So will the introduction of the new generation of powerful by-pass and ducted-fan turbojets if they

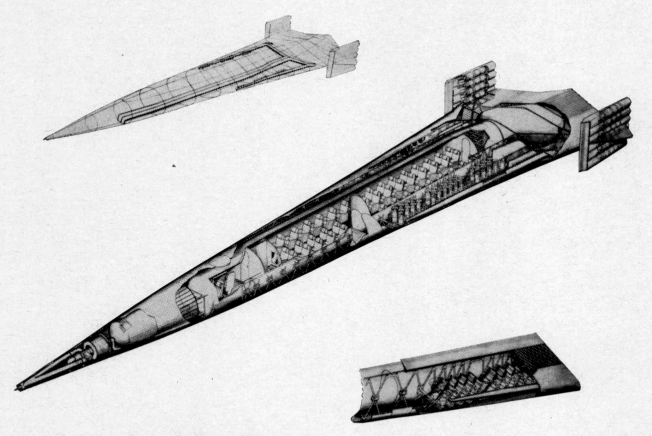

This dart-shape aircraft is probably the most advanced design for an airliner yet worked out in detail. Designed by Dr. A. A. Griffith of Rolls-Royce, it has batteries of small downward-pointing jet-engines to thrust it vertically off the ground at take-off. At a safe height, the main propulsion engines at the rear would begin to drive it forward. Its wings would then provide all necessary lift and the downward-pointing jets would be switched off until required for a vertical landing.

are used for this purpose instead of merely to increase speed in cruising flight. But it is to vertical take-off that we must look for the final, completely satisfactory and safe solution to this greatest of all airline problems.

Dr. A. A. Griffith of Rolls-Royce has given us an indication of what a supersonic VTO airliner might look like. Utilising the same basic idea as the Short S.C. 1 research aircraft, it is a huge delta-wing machine which is thrust off the ground vertically by batteries of small downward-pointing jet-engines. At a safe height the main rearward-facing engines

are gradually opened up to drive the aircraft forward: and when the wings develop sufficient lift to keep it airborne the downward-pointing jets are switched off.

Such an aircraft would need no long runways from which to operate, yet its cruising speed could be 1,000-m.p.h., 2,000-m.p.h. or anything of which its engine and airframe were capable. What is more, there is no reason why it should not be ready for service within ten years. So we need have no fear that future airline flying will be lacking in excitement.

THE BRISTOL SUPERFREIGHTER CAR FERRY: (1) Nose-opening car loading doors. (2) Cabin air-intake. (3) Cabin air duct sliding joint; connects when doors are closed. (4) Door operating hand wheel. (5) Door opening and closing mechanism. (6) Crew entry hatch. (7) Pilot and co-pilot. (8) Radio room. Operator on starboard side. (9) Warm air duct to passengers' cabin. (10) Cool air duct to passengers' cabin. (11) Car shackling chains round each wheel. (12) Car hold for three cars and several bicycles, or two cars and several motor-cycles and bicycles. (13) Port undercarriage. (14) Main spars of wings. (15) Eighteen-cylinder Bristol Hercules 734 radial engine, 2,000 h.p. (16) Cooling air fan. (17) Exhaust outlets. (18) Oil cooler. (19) Engine nacelle. (20) Inner port flap. (21) Outer port flap. (22) Port fuel tank, 136 gallons. (23) Port fuel tank, 100 gallons. (24) Wing de-icing strip. (25) Port taxi-ing light. (26) Port aileron; down, for aircraft banking to right. (27) Static electricity dischargers. (28) Large tail fin. (29) Rudder and trim tab. (30) Rudder controls. (31) Elevator controls. (32) Official attendant. (33) Cabin for 14 passengers. (34) Passengers' entrance door. (35) Tailplane de-icing strip. (36) Port elevator. (37) Swivelling tail wheel. (38) Starboard aileron; up.

THE COURSE OF 42 MILES ACROSS THE ENGLISH CHANNEL: (A) Outward flight at 1,000 ft. (B) Return flight at 2,000 ft. (C) Range of the British radar scanner, used for navigation in bad weather. (D) Range of the French radar scanner. Other car ferry services operate from Ferryfield, Lydd, to Calais and Ostend.

ARMSTRONG WHITWORTH ARGOSY: (1) Nose door open. This is the freight-loading end. (2) Radar, and crew's toilet. (3) Rearward-retracting nosewheels. (4) Freight hold (10 ft. wide by 47 ft. long). (5) Steps to flight deck. (6) Cargo lashing points. (7) Flight deck. (8) Captain's and co-pilot's seats. (9) Radar and radio operator's seat. (10) Radio racks. (11) Double skin of pressurised cabin. (12) Engine and flying controls, and automatic pilot. (13) Inner and outer starboard engines; Rolls-Royce *Dart* turboprops. (14) Inner port engine. (15) Jet outlet. (16) 11 ft. 6 in. diameter propellers. (17) Propeller reduction gear and air-compressors. (18) Combustion chambers to turbine wheels. In these engines, the turbine-driven propeller horse-power is all important; the jet thrust is of secondary importance. (19) Jet outlet of outer port engine. (20) Wing anti-icing warm-air pipes from jet exhaust. (21) Pressurised cabin air-pipe. (22) Bag-type fuel-tanks. Total capacity 3,300 gallons. (23) Rearward-retracting main undercarriage (under inner engines). (24) Double-slotted flaps. (25) Ailerons and trim tabs. (26) Static electricity dischargers. (27) Passenger entry door when aircraft is used for passenger carrying. (28) Rear door used for unloading. (29) Passenger baggage and toilet. (30) Elevator and rudder controls. (31)–(32) Twin tail-booms. (33) Elevators and trim tabs. (34)–(35) Twin tail-fins and rudders.

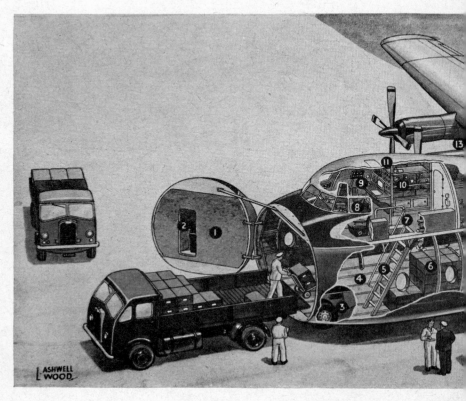

SILVER CITY
G-ANWK
L. ASHWELL WOOD.

it's 20 minutes to France

Greatest air cargo service in the world is Silver City's vehicle ferry across the English Channel to airfields in France and Belgium. In these pictures we see passengers checking in at Lydd (Ferryfield) Airport, their car being examined in the Customs hall and being loaded, with two others, into a Bristol Superfreighter ferryplane. At a signal from the control tower (*centre right*), the aircraft takes off, with the passengers seated comfortably in a cabin to the rear of the cargo hold. Within twenty minutes of take-off, they disembark at the colourful airport of Le Touquet in France.

What goes by Air?

JUST over thirty years ago, a number of birds took off from an airfield near London and flew to Paris. The birds—they were English grouse—were already trussed and ready for the oven, and therefore were not very interested in the journey. But they were making history.

The grouse, together with a pot of Devonshire cream and a solitary passenger, were being carried on the world's first regular commercial air service, and were thus almost certainly the first international consignment of cargo to travel on board an aircraft.

From this small beginning has grown an industry which can—and does—handle anything from a pin to a submarine. In fact, it is difficult to think of something that has not, at some time, or in some form, been carried by

When B.E.A. were asked to carry a submarine by air to Malta, for use in the film *The Silent Enemy*, they began to explain that even air freighting has its limitations. But all was well, because it turned out to be this small two-man submarine, which was packed easily into a Pionair-Leopard (DC-3) freighter.

It is true to say that almost everything which is not too big to go into an aeroplane, either whole or in sections, has been carried by air at some time or other, and some airlines do nothing but carry cargo. For them the manufacturers build aeroplanes with special nose or tail loading doors, for quick and easy loading.

Big advantage of a helicopter is that it can be used as a flying crane. Loads which are too big to go into its cabin can be picked up at the end of a cable while the aircraft hovers and then be carried externally, like this 27-ft. diameter radio telescope aerial under a Belvedere helicopter.

Another bulky load for the Belvedere is this Bloodhound anti-aircraft guided missile, on its transport trolley. Helicopters can carry smaller rockets or guns and their firing teams from point to point in a battle area for mobile "shoot and scoot" operations.

air. Even the proverbial "kitchen sink" has been airlifted—proof, surely, that the carriage of goods by air is now a major part of every-day aviation.

Freighting by air actually began long before aeroplanes were invented. The *Book of Animals*, written in the 14th century, tells how an ancient Vizier of Balbek in the Middle East, nearly a thousand years ago, heard that his master the Caliph of Cairo longed for some fresh cherries. So the Vizier obtained a "fleet" of 600 carrier pigeons, tied small bags each holding one cherry to their legs—and sent the fruit to Cairo by air!

Another early example of air freighting took place during the great siege of Paris by the Prussians in 1870. More than 9 tons of mail, 100 refugees and 400 carrier pigeons were flown out of the beleaguered capital by balloon. Many of the pigeons returned, carrying 100,000 messages photographed and reduced to a small size on microfilm.

The carriage of freight on a large scale developed only with the advent of modern aircraft of the post-1939–45 war era. However, even today air freighting is comparatively expensive and it must not be thought that the amount of freight carried by air in any way approaches the collossal amounts carried by rail, road or sea. For example, during the whole of 1959 all the freight that passed through London Airport totalled a mere 70,000 tons, which would hardly fill ten medium-size cargo boats. About twice this amount is unloaded *each day* at Britain's seaports.

The freight carried is usually of an urgent or perishable nature, so that the additional cost of sending it by air becomes worthwhile.

For example, when the New York office of a big shipping line received the following cable from Calcutta: "Engine breakdown. Urgently request ship turbine Calcutta. Signed S.S. *Devon Victory*", arrangements were immediately made to send by air the spare parts required. The cost was, perhaps,

£1,500; but the cost of wages, supplies, harbour charges and other expenses, would have totalled at least three times that amount had the spares been sent by sea.

On another occasion Silver City flew no fewer than 2,000 small components from Copenhagen to Bahrein for a ship that was swallowing up expenses in harbour at the rate of £800 a day.

Some ship's spare parts are quite big. The main engine turning wheel airlifted by Silver City to a stranded British tanker at Hamburg was 8 ft. 3 in. in diameter—5 in. wider than the hold of their Bristol Freighters—and weighed a ton. However, things like that are just part of the day's work for the cargo people and within a few hours a special frame had been made to support the wheel diagonally in the aircraft's freight hold.

Sometimes even the biggest 'plane cannot accommodate an urgently-needed piece of equipment, but that does not necessarily deter the airlines. Thus, when some 6½-ton propeller shafts were urgently needed in Singapore, British independent airline operators designed a special cradle to support them *underneath* the fuselage of their aircraft.

Fruit and flowers are good examples of perishable goods that are carried by air in large quantities. Air freighting brings the famous daffodils of the Scilly Isles to the mainland the same day they are picked, ensuring perfect freshness and longer life when they are bought to decorate our homes. In one year K.L.M. alone carried over 700 tons of Dutch flowers to other countries—and it takes a lot of flowers to weigh a ton.

The speed of air transport and reduced danger of theft *en route* makes air freighting an obvious choice for small, highly valuable consignments of gold and precious stones. In fact, Airwork flew the entire new currency of Jordan, consisting of banknotes, gold and silver coins, from Blackbushe to Mafrak in Jordan, after it had been minted and printed in England. When the currency was ready it

Part of one of the regular shipments of motor-cycles which are exported in batches of 20 on board Silver City Airways ferryplanes.

Its 16-ft. length did not prevent this canoe being carried by a de Havilland Otter, a sturdy transport used widely for "bush" flying in Canada.

Film-makers make extensive use of air transport, for time is often big money in their business. Here the first wide-screen Cinerama equipment is seen arriving at London Airport on board a Pan American World Airways flying freighter.

Air travel is so smooth that it is ideal for delicate cargoes like these replicas of Britain's Crown Jewels which were flown to Lima, Peru, for display at an international trade fair.

Typical of the awkward loads which air freighters are asked to handle was this package of repeater cable, airlifted for use in the under-the-Pacific telephone system.

Strange Air Cargo

Even ancient Romans fly. The owners of this 2,000-year-old bust had no fear that it would live up to its name if carried to New York on a B.O.A.C. cargo-plane.

This painting by a great artist was flown into London Airport by B.O.A.C. as part of one of the most valuable consignments of freight ever carried by air.

Well might this B.O.A.C. receptionist at London Airport ask, "What is it?" The object confronting her is a plastic model of the germ called "tobacco mosaic virus", destined for the University of California, San Francisco.

Few cargoes get a mayoral send-off, but this one was rather special. It consisted of a carved oak door for the Mayor's Parlour at Windsor, Ontario, and was sent as a gift from the people of Windsor, England.

This picture illustrates well how the speed of air transport often makes up for the higher cost of sending cargoes by air. It shows cigarette-making machinery on its way to Virginia, U.S.A. The air freight fare was very much higher than the comparable sea fare. But, on arrival at its destination, the machine was able to start work very much sooner. The money it earned during the period when it would normally have been crossing the Atlantic by boat more than offset the higher air fare.

Even ladies' dresses are air freighted in huge numbers, so that they can be got to the shops and sold before the fashion changes!

"Handle with care" is a request that applies particularly to irreplaceable links with the past such as this beautifully-preserved veteran car of 1908. B.E.A. airlifted it to Europe to take part in an international rally.

was rushed to the airport and put aboard the aircraft, where it was well out of the reach of potential thieves until it arrived at its destination, except for the short time spent refuelling on the way, when the aircraft were put under guard.

Unusual at first sight is the brisk trade in air freighting furniture. The reason is that often it is no dearer than surface transport, as no expensive packing is required and full insurance cover is included in the normal air freight charges.

Most remarkable furniture-lift was the occasion in America when Eastern Air Lines flew 100 tons of furniture from Miami to equip the £2½ million Caribe-Hilton Hotel in San Juan, Puerto Rico. Thirty aircraft were used to carry the 600 beds, 304 tallboys, 352 dressing-tables, 3,000 chairs and sofas, 355 standard lamps, carpets and other items.

In Europe, Silver City flew more than 200 roomsful of office equipment to France when the North Atlantic Treaty Organisation moved its headquarters from London to Paris.

Although the vast bulk of air cargo is

Yet another unusual load was this cigarette delivery van, complete with horse and coachmen, which was flown by Pan American from London to New York. More frequent, and much faster vehicle payloads are 180-m.p.h. Grand Prix racing cars, which are carried between races at even higher speeds than they achieve on the track.

composed of machinery and perishable and valuable goods of the kind described earlier, there is, in addition, a proportion of what can be described as strange cargo.

For example, the people of Malta would probably not have looked twice at a submarine surfacing in the capital's harbour—but their surprise can be imagined when one emerged from the hold of a B.E.A. Dakota! Also unusual was a package containing two spare bags and a supply of treacle lubricant, which was carried by B.O.A.C. to New York when the famous Dagenham Girl Pipers suffered from burst bagpipes.

Then there were the four boxes B.O.A.C. carefully loaded and then flew from London Airport, through San Francisco to Sydney, through India, the Middle East and back to London. When opened, the boxes were empty! The answer to this mystery was that the boxes, made of plywood, were being

tested for their ability to stand up to the rough handling received by a cargo packing case. On this trip the light and cheap test boxes returned in good condition.

Almost as strange was the 130-year-old lamp-post which B.O.A.C. flew to New York, the ultra-modern city of the world. No, the package was not incorrectly addressed, for the lamp-post, which had formerly stood in the shadow of Westminster Abbey, was to be erected in the New York British Book Centre to mark its tenth anniversary.

Another strange B.O.A.C. cargo was the celebrated cake, the largest ever made in Australia, which was flown to a British food fair. The cake was $13\frac{1}{2}$ ft. square, contained a hundredweight of sultanas, and was iced with a relief map of Australia.

That, even by the standards of a transport industry accustomed to surprises, surely takes the cake.

Noah's Arks of the Air

WHEN the Montgolfier brothers invented their hot-air balloon in 1783, the privilege of making the first aerial journey went to a duck, a sheep and a chicken! Since that time the number of animals travelling by air has increased rapidly, until today one passenger in every four carried by B.O.A.C. has four legs, feathers or fur.

The carrying of animals by air did not always go too well in the early days. In 1924,

This baby bull, carried by K.L.M. in 1924, was one of the first animals to travel in a Noah's Ark of the air. On the way it ate all the woodwork within reach in the cabin!

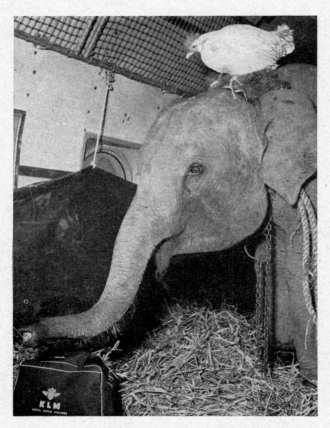

Even elephants fly—often. When they do a chicken usually goes along too, as animal stewards have found that elephants travel more contentedly in the company of a feathered friend.

Shipments of animals call for special treatment and all large airlines have a corps of highly trained "animal stewards". Experience in carrying animals has taught many lessons. Electric eels, for example, have to be carried in special insulated containers because they can generate a current of up to 350 volts. Zebras, antelopes, deer and similar beasts have to travel in boxes with sides padded to a depth of at least 12 in. to prevent them hurting themselves. Partridges and pheasants also need padded cells—they have a silly habit of jumping up and down violently and banging their heads on the roof. So cages for these usually have a piece of canvas stretched tightly across the top about 2 in. below the solid roof, to form a "crash barrier". Frogs, toads, newts and salamanders must always be kept damp, otherwise they cannot breathe through their skins and soon dry up and die.

The correct average temperature, humidity, atmospheric pressure and place inside aircraft have now been determined for each

for instance, the first bull to travel by air boarded a K.L.M. Royal Dutch Airlines airliner at Rotterdam. On arrival in Paris the bull looked exceedingly contented—which is hardly surprising, because during the trip it had eaten all the woodwork in the cabin!

The air transportation of live animals has made enormous strides since then and K.L.M. have played a leading part in this development. To ensure the safe carriage of horses, this airline has evolved special boxes which can be adjusted to fit any horse and which can also be converted into an aircraft gangway in a few seconds. One well-known horse to travel in one of these K.L.M. boxes was "Trigger", the mount of Roy Rogers of film and T.V. fame.

"This way, Sir, and have your Passport ready." The receptionist is smiling, but from the look on the performing chimpanzee's face, he is wondering if somebody is trying to make a monkey out of him.

species. An important point in this respect is the nature of the animal. A cage containing a tiger must never be placed near a cage of monkeys. One unusual discovery is that elephants travelling alone are put at ease and kept contented during a flight if a chicken is placed on their head!

One of the largest single loads carried in a flying Noah's Ark, a K.L.M. Skymaster, consisted of three elephants, one royal tiger, two tapirs, four pandas, 425 monkeys and 10,000 birds!

Another flying ark was the Pan American aircraft which landed with thirteen horned lizards, five gila monsters, two boa constrictors, a variety of other snakes, frogs, turtles, chameleons, sparrows, blue jays, robins, ten prairie dogs and two skunks.

The big advantage of sending such animals by air is that, compared with other forms of travel, they have to spend the fewest number of hours travelling through weather conditions differing from those experienced in their

The pilot oftens feels safer up on the flight deck when his load consists of such fierce-looking customers as these prize Shorthorns, which are being manœuvred into special pens designed to protect them during flight.

This falcon was one of four flown to Khartoum by B.O.A.C. Not all birds pay their fare. South African Airways, for example, carried 25 young wild swallows from Frankfurt to Rome, as they were too young to fly over the Alps themselves at migration time and would otherwise have died.

Goats waiting to board a K.L.M. "animal special" in Holland. Great care is taken of even the most humble beasts, and they have their own hostels, complete with medical centres, at some airports.

own country. If they come from a cold country they spend the shortest possible time travelling through the heat of the tropics. As a result they arrive at their destination in the finest possible condition. Air travel also tends to relax animals. Even thoroughbred racehorses, the most highly-strung and temperamental of all animals, cross oceans and continents quite happily by air and race within

This little girl was lucky enough to be first to ride "Trigger", the famous mount of cowboy film and T.V. star Roy Rogers, when it arrived at Prestwick Airport, Scotland, from New York.

a few hours of landing, whereas, after a long and perhaps rough sea crossing, they might require several weeks of rest.

One of the biggest livestock trades of all is between the Far East and Britain in tropical fish. The brilliantly coloured specimens which thrive in Singapore waters are in roaring demand among fish-keepers of the West, particularly in America. Unlike most of their fishy friends, hauled unexpectedly out of their watery homes in a net or on a hook, they are destined, not for the frying pan, but for a pampered life in the heated aquaria to be found in thousands of ordinary homes. Carried in plastic bags, and wrapped in insulated muffs to keep them warm, they swim unconcernedly half-way round the world to their new homes, no doubt finding one drop of water much like another, even when the drop is 20,000 ft. up and travelling at 6 miles a minute.

Among the other animals which travel by air on a large scale are one-day-old chickens which can be flown over huge distances with no ill effect. K.L.M. once carried 190,000 chicks from New York to Austria, where they the journey and could start to found a new colony with fresh energy on arrival in South America.

As is evident from the pictures illustrating this story, almost every kind of animal has travelled by air, except, perhaps, the giraffe. His neck seems to be too long even for the biggest freight aeroplanes yet made.

But this is the story we like best of all. An animal steward at La Guardia Airport, New York, took a husky animal of the sheep-dog variety for a walk during a refuelling

This seal, destined for London Zoo, leaves no doubt of his eagerness to get at his evening snack.

A dog's life has its compensations thinks "Belle", a Sealy-ham on its way to the United States.

were needed to reinforce the poultry stock. Speed is a most important factor in these cases, as the chickens must reach their destination within seventy-two hours if they are not to die of starvation. Special air conditioning is required for these shipments, both on the ground and in the air.

One interesting consignment, carried by B.O.A.C., was a box containing 40,000 fleas! Other Lilliputian travellers have included two Argentine queen ants with twenty consorts, and four queen bees accompanied by sixty worker bees. The bees were conveyed in special boxes made with honeycomb cells, so that the insects would not lay eggs during

stop. On the way he offered the animal a drink of water, which it proceeded to swallow in great thirsty sips. Another cargo man, who had been raised on a farm, commented that it was the first dog he had ever seen drinking water in that manner; he thought all dogs and other animals lapped water up with their tongues. In fact, the only sippers he knew in the animal kingdom were wolves! So, back into his crate went Brother Wolf in double quick time.

One wonders what the children—to whom the dog was being sent by an American soldier stationed in Germany—thought of their furry and sharp-toothed present!

VTOL and STOL

BACK in 1908 Thomas Alva Edison, the great inventor, was asked what he thought of the newly-invented aeroplane. He replied, "It won't amount to anything until they can get a machine that will act like a humming-bird—go straight up, go forward, go backward, come straight down and alight like a humming-bird." He added, "It isn't easy", and he was so right.

Today we have aircraft that can fly at 2,000 m.p.h. and even airliners that will carry 189 passengers from New York to London in 6½ hours. We also have helicopters and several other types of VTOL (vertical take-off and landing) aircraft that will do everything Edison demanded. What we still have to do is find a way of combining the best features of both the conventional fixed-wing aeroplane and the VTOL types—and it still isn't easy!

The reasons for wanting to take off vertically have already been explained so far as civil aircraft are concerned. In the case of military aircraft, VTOL flight dispenses with

This must be just about the costliest way of getting a motor car from one place to another, but the object was to demonstrate that there are few objects with a weight under 6 tons that cannot be carried by the big Sikorsky S-60 Skycrane helicopter. To permit the greatest possible payload, the aircraft's structure has been reduced to a minimum. It consists simply of a "backbone" carrying the twin engines, rotor system and a small cabin at the front for the two-man crew. The co-pilot's seat swivels so that he can face backward and supervise the loading and unloading of cargoes while the Skycrane is hovering.

the need for difficult-to-build, easy-to-locate-and-destroy concrete runways, and means that aircraft can be operated from anywhere, even front-line areas in rough country. As a result, there is no class of aircraft that would not benefit from the ability to take off and land vertically. What, then, are the problems?

Basically, they result from the fact that whilst an aeroplane needs less than 150 h.p. to take off normally and carry four people at a cruising speed of 125 m.p.h., it must have three times as much power if it also has to be capable of vertical take-off in the form of a helicopter. This makes a helicopter much more expensive to buy and to run than a fixed-wing aeroplane. Furthermore, the helicopter's rotating wing limits its forward speed to little more than 220-m.p.h., beyond which the tips of the blades turn so fast that they begin to run into "sound barrier" problems.

Whatever we do to the ordinary straight-forward helicopter, these drawbacks will always remain. However, there are many jobs which do not require a speed greater than 220 m.p.h. In any case, a 200-m.p.h. helicopter could fly directly from the centre of London to the centre of Paris far more quickly than a passenger could do the same trip by the present combination of airline coaches and 500-m.p.h. jet-liner.

Other kinds of work are such that they offset the high costs of operating a helicopter. For example, thousands of lives have been saved by helicopters which have hovered over wrecked ships or buildings threatened by rising floods and lifted the occupants to safety on the end of a rescue hoist. Any cost is cheap compared with a human life.

There are countless other jobs on which the helicopter saves so much time and effort that it more than pays its way. Examples include flying oil-men between the coast and off-shore drilling rigs, carrying dam-building equipment to sites high in the mountains, spraying chemicals over valuable farm crops

This dramatic picture shows a Vertol HUP helicopter of the U.S. Navy rescuing a pilot from the sea within seconds of his crashing over the side of an aircraft carrier. Hundreds of lives have been saved in this way.

Latest life-saving duty for helicopters is for fire-fighting. This Kaman H-43B Huskie can haul a large extinguisher and firemen to a crashed aircraft far more quickly than a normal fire-engine, and can beat down the flames with its rotors.

Even small helicopters can be used as flying cranes. The rotor of this French Djinn is turned by simply ejecting compressed air from blade-tip nozzles, as a garden sprinkler is turned by water pressure.

that are being attacked by insect pests, and inspecting power-lines for damage in rough or wooded country.

Sometimes the helicopter can even offer a clear saving in cash by dispensing with the need for roads when an experimental mining base has to be set up in the middle of a jungle, or by using its ability to operate as a "flying crane" to unload ships where there is no harbour, or by hoisting a heavy piece of equipment to the top of a high building without the need for costly scaffolding. At one time such tasks were regarded as mere stunts; but today they are quite normal operations and a helicopter company shows no surprise if it is asked to hoist an angel to the top of a church tower or drop a series of telegraph poles

into concrete-packed holes in places which are inaccessible to other forms of transport.

Whatever happens in the future, it seems safe to say that there will always be jobs that helicopters will do better than anything else. Their design will continue to improve, and piston-engines are already giving way to more efficient shaft-turbines (turboprops which drive the rotor instead of a propeller) and various forms of tip-drive. The latter in the case of the French Djinn lightweight two-seater consists of simply squirting compressed-air from nozzles at the tips of the rotor blades, so that the rotor is turned in the same way that a garden sprinkler is turned by water pressure. In other cases, where higher power is needed, air is mixed with fuel and burned in simple ramjet or pressure-jet engines carried on the blade-tips.

This brings us to the Rotodyne 54/75-seat airliner, which represents one of the greatest advances yet made in rotating-wing flight. It can best be regarded as a twin-engined airliner in which the outer half of each wing has been cut off and a four-blade rotor fitted to make up for the loss of wing area and lift. The other basic change is that its turboprops can be geared to drive either the normal forward-facing propellers or an auxiliary compressor at the rear of each engine. This compressor pumps air up through the hollow rotor blades to pressure-jets on the tips.

During take-off and landing, the Rotodyne is a pure helicopter. The turboprops are used to drive the auxiliary compressors and the rotor is turned by the pressure-jets. When a safe height has been reached, the aircraft begins to fly forward, still as a helicopter, until it is moving fast enough for the wings to provide about half the lift required to keep it airborne. The auxiliary compressors are then de-clutched, which stops the pressure-jets and leaves the rotor windmilling freely in the airflow, and the power of the turboprops is used to drive the propellers in the normal way.

These pictures show well the versatility of modern helicopters. *Above*, a Hiller 12E three-seater demonstrates its manœuvrability. The much larger, twin-turbine Sikorsky HSS-2 (*below left*) is amphibious. A Whirlwind (*below right*) shows its strength by towing the 360-ton minesweeper *Gavinton*.

World's first vertical take-off airliner is the British Rotodyne, designed to carry up to 75 passengers on city centre services. It is also the world's fastest rotorcraft, and holds the international speed record of 191 m.p.h. over a 62-mile course.

In cruising flight, therefore, the Rotodyne is little different from a fixed-wing airliner, except that about half its lift continues to be provided by the rotor. The big advantage is that the rotor is used most of the time only to provide lift (instead of lift and forward thrust, as in a helicopter), so that it is lightly-loaded and does not turn so fast that it runs into trouble. This enables the Rotodyne to cruise at more than 220 m.p.h., which is beyond the capabilities of an ordinary helicopter.

Of course, the idea of using an unpowered rotor is not new. The very first successful rotating-wing aircraft, Cierva's Autogiros of the 1920's and 30's, worked like the Rotodyne in cruising flight, with an engine and propeller to provide forward thrust and a "free-wheeling" rotor to provide lift. But an Autogiro is not really capable of vertical take-off and hovering. A drive-shaft from the engine can be engaged temporarily to start the rotor turning on the ground and permit a "jump-start" to about 50 ft., but the Autogiro is an STOL (short take-off and landing) rather than VTOL type.

Because it converts from a helicopter to an Autogiro in the air, the Rotodyne is what is known as a convertiplane. This term is used to cover any kind of machine that changes its configuration in this way, and no class of aircraft contains a more varied or strange collection of shapes and sizes.

The Rotodyne is a fairly complicated piece of machinery and several attempts are being made to achieve the same kind of result more simply.

Most promising is perhaps the tilt-wing aircraft, of which the Hiller X-18 is a good example. This is basically a quite conventional twin-engined aeroplane, but the whole wing can be turned through 90 degrees. This enables the specially-designed propellers to work as rotors during vertical take-off, hovering and landing, and as normal propellers in cruising flight. It is not quite so simple as this. Cross-shafts have to be provided, so that one engine can drive both propellers if the other fails. And a jet-engine has had to be mounted in the rear fuselage, with a long tail-pipe and upward- and downward-pointing nozzles, to provide pitch control during vertical and low-speed flight when the elevators are not effective.

The wing-tilting mechanism of the X-18 is fairly weighty, but this is offset by the advantages. The absence of rotors means that there is no limit of around 220 m.p.h. on forward speed, and the X-18 can take off with its wing in the normal position when runways are available, carrying an increased load. With the wing in an intermediate position it becomes an STOL type.

In the Bell XV-3 convertiplane, it is only the rotor/propellers that tilt, not the whole wing. A variation of this idea is used in the Doak VZ-4DA, in which the XV-3's large-diameter rotors are replaced by what are called ducted fans. These consist of rotor/propellers turning inside barrel-shape ducts, which so increase the efficiency of the propellers that they give as much lift as un-ducted propellers of far greater diameter.

Ducted fans can be used in several other

A competitor for the heli-copter as a transport vehicle able to take off and land vertically is the Hiller X-18 tilt-wing aeroplane. As can be seen in this sequence of pictures, its entire wing can be tilted through 90 degrees, so that the propellers of its two 5,850-h.p. turboprop en-gines work as helicopter rotors during take-off and landing. During these phases, the normal tail controls are ineffective; so the fuselage is kept on an even keel by ejecting the exhaust of a small jet-engine through upward and downward pointing noz-zles under the aircraft's tail. At a safe height the wing is gradually tilted down and the X-18 cruises as a perfectly normal twin-engined aero-plane. The big advantage com-pared with helicopters is that the absence of a rotor in cruising flight permits much higher forward speeds, but the tilt-wing aircraft is fairly complicated mechanically.

Here are three more types of VTOL aircraft. The Doak VZ-4DA (*top left*) is something like a tilt-wing aeroplane, except that only the ducted propellers on the ends of its wings are tilted. Another variation is the Bell XV-3 convertiplane (*left*) which has tilting rotors instead of the ducted propellers of the Doak. Far more startling at first sight is the Hiller Flying Platform (*above*) which the pilot steers by leaning in the direction he wants to travel.

ways. In the little Hiller VZ-1E Flying Platform, the pilot stands above a ducted fan and simply leans in the direction he wants to go: the rotor then gives thrust as well as lift, like that of a helicopter.

Two ducted rotors are used in the Piasecki VZ-8P Flying Jeep, which will do anything

First of a series of Flying Jeeps built for the U.S. Army was this Piasecki VZ-8P, in which the pilot and passengers sit between two large ducted rotors. A four-seat civil version named the Sky-Car is being designed.

of which its land-based counterpart is capable without needing to worry about obstructions like rivers or mountains: but in this case control is by hinged vanes under the ducts instead of by slight tilting of the rotors.

Several of the hovercraft or GEM's (ground effect machines) now under test look rather like the VZ-8P, but they operate on entirely different principles. The VZ-8P is a variation of the helicopter and can fly high above the ground. This increases its usefulness compared with a low-flying hovercraft, but means that it needs as much power as a helicopter. The pioneer British Hovercraft, on the other hand, has demonstrated its ability to carry twenty fully-equipped troops, in addition to its pilot, on only 450-h.p.—the same power as a five-seat helicopter. It does so by making use of the "ground-cushion effect".

The easiest way to picture a simple hovercraft is as a kind of large saucepan-lid, with a horizontal rotor mounted in a hole in the middle. The rotor flings down air, forming a cushion of air under the lid, and this supports the aircraft just clear of the ground. Some of the air leaks out between the edge of the lid and the ground, but this is replaced continuously and the hovercraft simply rides along on the cushion, tilting itself slightly or deflecting the air by means of vanes to provide directional control.

Several aircraft now flying are no more complicated than this, but Britain's Hovercraft is more advanced in that the air is ejected in the form of two "curtains" around the perimeter of the "lid". These curtains are powerful enough to prevent most of the air cushion inside them from leaking out, and air losses are small. This type is, therefore, more efficient, especially for large aircraft, and we can expect to see a lot more of the hovercraft in the years ahead. It is useful only when the surface over which it has to move is fairly flat, as it flies so close to the ground or water; but a very large hovercraft would be capable of crossing the Atlantic at 100 m.p.h., carrying passengers, cars and freight more cheaply than any other form of vehicle.

Every type of VTOL aircraft described so far utilises some kind of rotor or propeller to provide its lift. When higher speeds are needed, there is no reason at all why jet thrust should not be used instead, as in fixed-wing aircraft. One aeroplane that does so is the Short S.C. 1, described at the beginning of this book, and some designers believe that one day jet-lift of this kind will be used by a high proportion of all fast or large aircraft. Nor need the downward-pointing engines be used only during take-off or landing, and be carried as dead weight the rest of the time. They can be made to tilt like the ducts of the Doak VZ-4DA, or be fitted with "eyelid" jet-deflector nozzles, which bend downward through 90 degrees the jet-efflux of normally-mounted engines to provide jet-lift during take-off and landing. The Hawker P. 1127 VTOL fighter uses this principle.

One thing we must remember, however, is that even the most efficient form of VTOL technique costs something in terms of extra power requirements or reduced payload. It is worthwhile only when it increases an aircraft's safety or usefulness, and many experts believe that the STOL aeroplane is more practical for many everyday jobs. They point

(Continued on page 96)

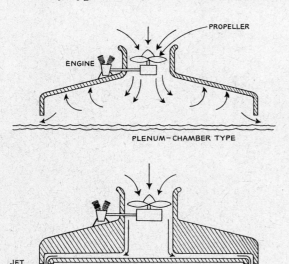

PLENUM—CHAMBER TYPE

JET CURTAIN

ANNULAR JET

Hovercraft make use of the principle that comparatively little power is needed to raise a vehicle clear of the ground on an air cushion, provided you don't need to fly more than a few inches high. The simplest kind of hovercraft are of the plenum-chamber type, in which the air cushion is simply blown down by a propeller and is allowed to leak away continuously all round the edge. Britain's pioneer SR-N1 Hovercraft (above) is of the annular jet type, in which the air is ejected in the form of curtains around the edge of the vehicle. These curtains prevent most of the cushion air from leaking away and the result is a more efficient machine.

NEW YORK BY HELICOPTER

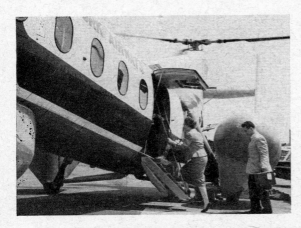

The only way to appreciate fully the mighty grandeur of the skyscraper city of New York is to see it from the air. This is easy now, for New York Airways operate regular sightseeing services with Vertol helicopters.

Leaving the Manhattan Heliport (*bottom of opposite page*), we whirr along the East River, against a backdrop of the tallest buildings in the world. We get a grandstand view of the impressive United Nations Building (*bottom right*), with the Chrysler Building, second only to the Empire State Building, in the background. Cruising on down the Hudson River, we pass the Statue of Liberty, before turning west towards Newark Airport, in New Jersey. This is a view of the famous statue (*below*) which few of New York's millions have ever enjoyed.

95

Fairchild's Model M-224-1 experimental STOL aeroplane shows that helicopters are not the only craft able to take off vertically, during early tethered tests. It gets its vertical lift by blowing back air from four large-diameter propellers over huge wing flaps.

out that there are few places where a military force could not level out a 500-yard landing strip, and an STOL fighter or bomber operating from such a strip would be faster and carry a heavier load of weapons than a comparable VTOL type. That is why a great deal of effort is being put into aircraft with huge wing flaps and slots, "flap-blowing" systems, and large-diameter propellers, the slipstream from which increases lift over the entire wing surface.

All kinds of other ideas are likely to be tried out in the next ten years. Rockets are already being used to help fighters and bombers get into the air more quickly with a heavy load, and the Bell Helicopter Corporation has completed design studies of huge nuclear-powered VTOL aircraft for the U.S.A.F. A 250-ton atomic-engined helicopter, almost as long as a football field, might seem to have little in common with Thomas Alva Edison's humming-bird; but it would do everything he asked and a lot more, beyond the old man's most fabulous dreams.

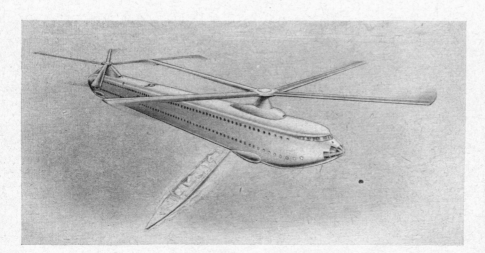

Whatever new forms of VTOL and STOL aircraft are developed, many experts believe there will always be a place for the helicopter. One possible glimpse of the future is given by this drawing of a mighty 250-ton atomic-powered helicopter designed by the Bell company under a U.S.A.F. study contract. With a length of 300 ft., it could carry many hundreds of passengers or immense weights of cargo over unlimited ranges at a speed of 200 m.p.h. There is no plan at present to build the big aircraft, but it opens up exciting possibilities.

THE HILLER ROTORCYCLE
A ONE-MAN HELICOPTER

How would you like to have your own little one-man helicopter, small enough to pack into the back of a station wagon, yet capable of carrying you anywhere at more than 50 m.p.h.? Such a craft is already flying, in the form of the Hiller Rotorcycle, a folding helicopter designed originally for the U.S. Marines which is small enough to be dropped by parachute to soldiers in the field, and simple enough to be assembled by one man in a matter of minutes. The folding parts are secured in place by inserting only 13 standard quick-release pins, one of which is being pushed into place in the picture at the top right of this page.

The Rotorcycle is powered by a 43-h.p. Nelson H-63B two-stroke engine, which drives an 18 ft. 6 in. diameter two-blade main rotor. It weighs only 300 lb. and has a normal range of 166 miles. Top speed is 70 m.p.h.

Learning to Fly

THE easiest and cheapest way to learn to fly is to join the Combined Cadet Force or, alternatively, the Air Training Corps. All A.T.C. cadets are given an opportunity to learn gliding; the best and keenest can also receive free training on powered aeroplanes up to the standard required for a Private Pilot's Licence.

A glider is controlled in the same way as a powered aircraft, but as it has no engine to pull it along, it must always glide downhill in order to obtain sufficient forward speed for the wings to develop the required lift. This is true even when a glider is gaining height—it is actually descending through the air, but as the surrounding air is rising at a faster rate its height above the ground actually increases. It is rather like walking down an up-going escalator.

Careful finish and design enable a glider to fly downhill only at a very flat angle to maintain flying speed. This downward path is known as the Gliding Angle, and on the average glider it is about one in twenty-four. This means that if a glider is a mile up, it is able to fly a distance of 24 miles in still air before landing. With practice, gliders can do aerobatics, can be landed in small, confined places, and can be flown in calm or rough weather.

Typical of the training gliders on which pupils are taught to fly is this two-seat Slingsby Cadet Mk. 3 of No. 48 A.T.C. Gliding School. It is simply constructed of wood, covered with fabric, and is very easy to control. The knowledge of flying, and especially of air currents, gained in motorless flight is of untold value to anyone who later becomes a pilot of powered aircraft. That is why the Government encourages young people to fly through the Air Training Corps and Combined Cadet Force.

Members of the Royal Air Force section of the C.C.F. receive preliminary gliding training, and usually begin on an elementary but sturdy glider supported on a stand, so that it can tilt and bank in a slight wind and so enable cadets to get used to the feel of the controls.

If you begin as an A.T.C. cadet, you will start off in a more spectacular fashion. After an introductory series of lectures on elementary aerodynamics and the theory of flight, you will probably climb into a two-seat Slingsby Sedbergh glider beside your instructor and then, without any preliminary ground slide or hop—whoosh—up to 1,000 ft. you will go.

You will then make about six more flights to get to know the effect of control movements and to learn the various gliding techniques.

After this you will change on to another glider, probably the Kirby Cadet Mk. 3, in which you'll sit in front of the instructor. In this you'll make several more flights and, as you become more and more proficient, the instructor will guide you less and less until you are flying it all by yourself.

But before you go solo you will be carefully checked to ensure that you know how to:

Recover from a cable break or winch failure at difficult heights.

Regain control of your glider from unusual attitudes.

Recover from an inadvertent spin.

If you are able to overcome these three emergencies, then after a few more flights on the Cadet Mk. 3 you will be ready for one of the most exciting days of your life. You will go up by yourself for your first solo!

(*Continued on page 102*)

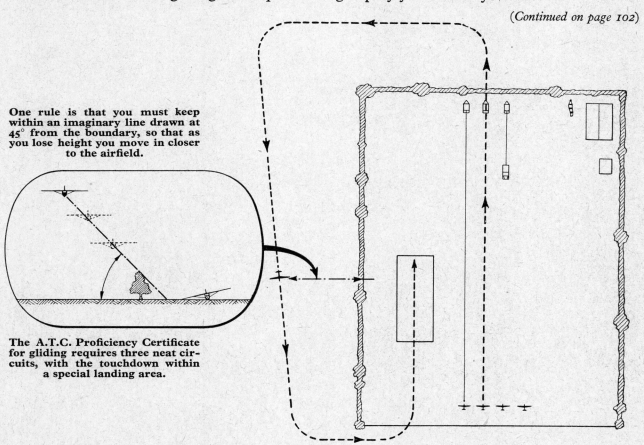

One rule is that you must keep within an imaginary line drawn at 45° from the boundary, so that as you lose height you move in closer to the airfield.

The A.T.C. Proficiency Certificate for gliding requires three neat circuits, with the touchdown within a special landing area.

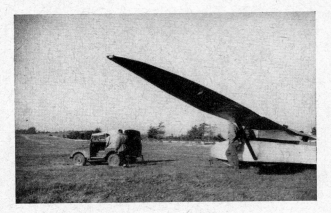

1. The tow to the take-off point. The person steadying the fuselage would be more alert if his hand was free from his pocket.

Gliding, although simple, is safe only if all the rules are obeyed all the time. The following photographs cover the sequence of events for a typical circuit, and show you some of the things that you ought to do—and some of the things you shouldn't.

Note: Several different kinds of glider are shown in this series of pictures. See if you can identify them. The answers are given at the foot of page 102.

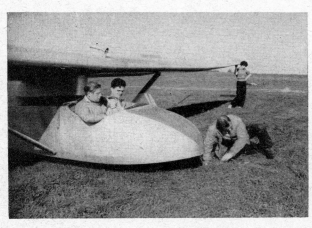

2. At first glance, the person kneeling appears to be hooking on the tow rope. He shouldn't be—for this action does not take place until the pilots are securely strapped in.

3. Waiting for the cable. The wing tip orderly appears to be half sitting on the wing. Unless he is careful this could damage the wing.

4. Checking the tow rope. This is a "vital" action, and the hook must always be examined for excessive wear, that might prevent it releasing properly. This check is not normally carried out with the dive brakes extended—the aircraft should be "clean" and ready for flight.

5. Almost ready to go—but someone is ignoring a "vital" rule. The person at the tail is too close to the rudder and elevators and could damage them when the pilot operates the controls, or if the glider develops a swing at the start of the take-off.

6. Really ready to go, and this time all is correct. Or is that left wing a little low?

7. "Take up slack." The winch operator winds the cable in slowly until it is taut with the glider. . . .

8. "All Out." The signaller waves his bat over his head and the winch operator opens the throttle wide.

9. Within a few seconds the glider is airborne. Notice that in this picture, taken on a different occasion to the previous one the signaller is using two bats.

10. Climbing steadily. This is a critical stage and at this height the pupil must resist the temptation to climb too steeply, otherwise in the event of cable failure the aircraft may stall with insufficient height for recovery.

There are four main methods of getting gliders into the air: aero-towing, car-towing, catapulting and winch launching. Aero-towing, easy and safe, is probably the best as it can take you to any desired altitude. If, however, you learn to glide with either the C.C.F. or the A.T.C., you will most probably be launched by a winch, as shown in the picture below. An advantage of this method is that launching can be carried out over rough ground.

11. Well up on the launch.

12. Friends of the pilot watch critically as he banks and turns before coming in to land. Much can be learned in this way by studying the actions of others.

After more practice you will go in for the Proficiency Certificate, for which you have to make three neat circuits, two in one direction and one the opposite way, landing each time in an area measuring 50 by 200 yards.

If you show promise and are keen, you may have further instruction in aerobatics, looping and stall turns, followed by aero-towing, during which you are towed off the ground by a powered aircraft.

When you can remain above the point of release for fifteen minutes you qualify for the Advanced Certificate.

These Royal Air Force Certificates require a high standard, and if you obtain them you qualify automatically for the A, B and C Certificates of the Royal Aero Club. The A Certificate normally requires a "high hop" and glide lasting about thirty seconds; the B requires two curved glides lasting forty-five seconds and one flight of sixty seconds. The C Certificate requires a soaring flight of five minutes above the point of cable release.

After a lot more flying experience you may join a civilian or R.A.F. gliding club and attempt to obtain the International Silver C Certificate. To qualify for this you have to fly a distance of 32 miles, climb to 3,200 ft., and remain airborne for five hours. You do not have to do all three on one flight; they may be achieved at intervals on separate occasions.

The next certificate, the Gold C, is far more difficult to get. For this a pilot has to cover a distance of nearly 200 miles, and climb more than 10,000 ft.

Finally, the really outstanding pilot can add Diamonds to his Gold C, by gliding 300 miles to a declared landing goal and climbing to 16,000 ft.

Of course, not many readers will ever obtain this coveted award. But even weekend club gliding can be great fun. One of the best things about gliding is that you can learn at any age—provided your feet can reach the rudder pedals—although you cannot fly solo until you are sixteen.

Did you recognise the gliders correctly?

1. Sedbergh T21B; 2. Sedbergh T21B; 3. Cadet Mk. 3 T31 Tandem Tutor; 4. Eon Olympia; 5. Cadet Mk. 3 T31 Tandem Tutor; 6. Sedbergh T21B; 7. Sedbergh T21B; 8. Sedbergh T21B; 9. Slingsby Prefect; 10. Cadet Mk. 3 T31 Tandem Tutor; 11. Sedbergh T21B; 12. Sedbergh T21B.

Aviation in Miniature

Almost all readers of this *Eagle New Book of Aircraft* must have made up some of the excellent plastic model air- craft kits that are now available. These kits are remarkable value for their relatively low cost, and enable nearly anyone to turn out a model

A fine Revell model of the Convair F-102A Delta Dagger supersonic interceptor.

Rockets are not overlooked; this is a Nike Hercules anti- aircraft missile kit.

Nearly 80 carefully-moulded pieces make up this Airfix authentic 1/72nd scale model of a Bristol Superfreighter.

This de Havilland Heron kit includes a retractable undercarriage, movable control surfaces, crew, passengers and flight steps.

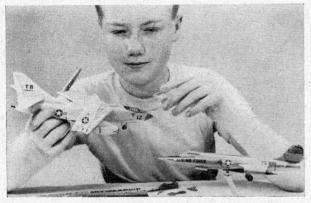
This boy is holding a Douglas A3D Skywarrior model he has just completed. In the foreground is a Lockheed F-104 Starfighter.

which, a few years ago, would have taken a skilled craftsman weeks of painstaking work to equal.

The models are not "toys"; they are scientific scale replicas of the full-size prototypes they represent, and their accuracy is now legendary. When Revell planned their Lockheed F-104 Starfighter model, their engineers hunted for information so diligently that when they forwarded the mould drawings to Lockheed for checking, they were *too* authentic. They were classified as secret until the Air Force cleared the relevant details a month later. On another occasion, when Revell decided to produce a model of the then secret Russian Yak-25 jet fighter, photos and details were carefully collected from all available sources, but nothing reliable could be obtained of the landing gear mechanism. Relying on their study of other Russian aircraft, Revell's engineers designed the Yak's undercarriage as they imagined the Russians would. Several months later an officially-released Russian photograph proved the Revell design correct in all basic details.

Scale models offer hours of enjoyment, but for the summer evenings there is nothing to equal flying models. Each year nation-wide rallies are held, at which aero-modellers compete for trophies, including the Queen Elizabeth Cup, given by the Queen Mother as the junior equivalent of the famous King's Cup for full-size aeroplanes. The Queen Elizabeth Cup is open only to powered models, but the average big flying meeting usually includes contests for solid scale models, gliders, rubber-driven models, petrol, diesel, jet and rocket-powered aircraft, racers, duration models—a bewildering variety of shapes, sizes and types more numerous than even their full-scale counterparts.

Best known of all aviation models are those used in wind tunnels to help develop the aerodynamics of full-size aircraft. Such models are made by the finest craftsmen, because they must be accurate to one-

This 17-ft. wing-span model was made to assist the development of the radio installation of the Convair 880. On this jet airliner the aerials are patterned on those used on supersonic military aircraft; the top 4 ft. of the fin will act as the aerial used to send and receive messages.

hundredth of an inch if their performance in the wind tunnel is to be of any value to the chief designer and his aerodynamicists. Some are beautifully made of polished wood with no added detail; but sometimes even these superb models are not good enough and metal models, accurate to 1/1,000th in. are used instead. Others are almost as complicated as a lightplane, with electrically driven propellers, control surfaces and undercarriages that can be raised and lowered from a control panel outside the tunnel.

Even more remarkable are the "dynamically similar" free flight models. These are supreme examples of the model-maker's art, for not only are they perfect replicas of their full-size counterparts, but are built so that the major parts of their structure are to scale in weight, as well as size and shape. Consequently, by fitting them with miniature petrol-engines and flying them under radio-control, designers can study their behaviour to a degree not attainable in a wind tunnel.

It is impossible to exaggerate the importance of these research models, for, by indicating a serious fault in the early stages of design, they can not only save a lot of time and money, but perhaps even the life of a test pilot. Things like emergency cockpit hood jettison, the behaviour of a fighter if its two underwing fuel tanks fail to drop clear at the same moment, or the flow of air into the engine intakes of a civil airliner, can be tested in a wind tunnel far more easily, cheaply and safely than in flight on a real aeroplane, and the results are incredibly accurate.

Among the most important of all models are those built to test the ability of full-scale aircraft to alight on the water in an emergency without breaking-up or turning over. Their structure has to be a perfect replica of the actual aircraft, not only in shape but in comparative strength, so that if it buckles the designer will know that the full-size version would also break. This picture shows a model of the Short Britannic freighter, which has been catapulted into a ditching tank on the Isle of Wight

More ditching tests, this time with a model of the American Project Mercury manned satellite capsule. After orbital flights in space, the astronaut will slow down, re-enter the atmosphere, and eventually descend in his capsule under a large parachute. It is planned to end the trip in the ocean, and this picture, showing a model capsule at intervals as it approaches the water, indicates that it should make a reasonably smooth impact.

Surely one of the largest models ever built, this half-scale Canberra was made by Westway Models of Acton for exhibition at an air show in Paris. Another British company built a full-scale non-flying replica of the Vickers Vimy for use in a film of the first non-stop Atlantic flight by Alcock and Brown. Unfortunately, work on the film was stopped just as it was completed but, like this Canberra, it showed that model-makers are seldom deterred by the size of a job they are asked to undertake.

Do-it-yourself Lightplanes

A FEW years ago a shopkeeper in America decided to build the world's biggest flying model aeroplane, as a stunt. When he had finished it, he realised that it was big enough to fly in. So he fitted a seat, controls and engine, and was soon happily airborne.

Few other lightplanes can have had such a remarkable history, but the idea of building one's own aeroplane is not new. Santos-

Two lightweight "home-builts" from France. That illustrated above was the first aeroplane ever designed to be built and flown by amateurs—Santos-Dumont's *Demoiselle*. The other machine is Henri Mignet's ill-fated "Flying Flea".

Dumont designed a tiny "do-it-yourself" machine called the *Demoiselle* in 1908, and several were built and flown without killing their pilots. Unfortunately, they were well before their time, as aviators were still regarded as supermen and the public had little ambition to leave the ground.

A quarter of a century later another designer in France tried to produce an aeroplane that anyone could afford to build and everyone could fly. He named it the Flying Flea and it lived up to its name when he demonstrated it. Before long Fleas were being mass-produced by would-be fliers all over the world, and the only snag was that few of them were content to stick to the original design. Some tried to introduce "improvements" of their own; others were none too fussy about the standard of their workmanship. As a result, several Fleas crashed and others refused to leave the ground, which was perhaps as well. Eventually the design was banned and another "do-it-yourself" phase ended.

The Second World War had been over only a few years when the idea was again revived in France, and this time it was a case of third time lucky. The main reason was that the people who designed the new generation of "home-builts" did not try to be too venturesome. They chose a conventional low-wing monoplane layout, and fitted well-proven power plants like the American 65-h.p. Continental or modified versions of the Volkswagen motor-car engine. So well did their little machines fly that the French Government decided to pay some of the cost of those which were built and flown successfully by amateurs, and this encouraged thousands of young people to take an interest in flying.

The same kind of thing is happening in America, under the guidance of the Experimental Aircraft Association. All kinds of interesting little machines turn up at its annual fly-ins, and big prizes are awarded for the cleverest designs capable of being built by people with little previous experience. It also

This picture of German manufacturer Hubert Zuerl with one of his Jodel D.11C two-seater kits shows how little work the amateur constructor need do if he has no ambition to start from scratch.

Marcel Jurca's Tempête is a real "junior Spitfire", able to fly at 120 m.p.h. on only 65 h.p. He has sold plans of it to would-be constructor-pilots all over the world.

Many home-builders prefer the racey lines of a biplane, and the little Smith Miniplane is being constructed in large numbers in America. Although easy to fly, it is no toy and can be used for spirited aerobatics.

Although they can be classed as home–builts, the three aircraft on this page are very different from the usual do–it–yourself types. *Miss Dara* (*above*) is a midget racer, built to a strict set of rules which ensure that races are won by the skill of designers and pilots rather than by sheer power or unsafe design. It can fly at around 200 m.p.h. on only 85 h.p. Jerry Lawhorn's *Kee Bird* (*right*) was built for use in Alaska, hence the huge balloon tyres for smooth landings on rough ground. Below it is the 86-in. span Stits Skybaby, world's smallest aeroplane. Despite its tiny size, it flew successfully.

maintains close links with the Professional Race Pilots Association, whose members build and race around pylons beautifully-streamlined little aircraft which get a speed of over 200 m.p.h. from engines of only 85 h.p.

Life is less easy for would-be amateur builders in Britain. The Popular Flying Association does its best to help; but there are fewer aerodromes at which lightplanes are welcomed and the whole country is criss-crossed with a network of airway "sky tunnels" for airliners, into which private 'planes may not venture. Nevertheless, several French-designed Turbulents and Turbis have been completed by enthusiasts, and even one or two lightplanes of original design.

Something new in flying-boats is the Bensen Gyro-Boat, seen here above a motor-boat and water-skier. When towed behind a fast boat, it is kept in the air by its wind-milling two-blade rotor.

Most unusual of the "home-builts" are the Gyro-Copters—baby Autogiros of which plans and kits of parts can be bought from the Bensen Company in America. These started off as unpowered Gyro-Glider rotor-kites, which become airborne, with their rotor wind-milling to provide lift, when they are towed behind a motor-car.

Even boys of twelve to fifteen have built and flown Gyro-Gliders, because no licence is required to pilot unpowered aircraft. When they become older, they can fit an engine and propeller, and the aircraft is then a Gyro-Copter. There are all sorts of other variations of the basic rotor-kite, and Bensen have given a new meaning to the term "flying-boat" by fitting Gyro-Gliders to dinghies, so that they can be towed over water behind a fast motor-boat. So, if you ever look out of the porthole of a ship and see a boat flash past 20 ft. above the water, there will be no need to send for a psychiatrist or eye-specialist. The chances are it will simply mean that somebody else has discovered the cheapest, easiest way of getting himself airborne.

These little home-built Bensen Gyro-Copter Autogiros are just the job for getting to an out-of-the-way spot for a day's fishing. Easy to make and fly, they will go 120 miles in 2 hours on 5 gallons of fuel.

How an Aircraft is Born

IN the very early days of aviation, aeroplanes were often designed and built by one or two men in a few weeks. If they didn't work they were simply pulled to pieces, altered, rebuilt and tried out again until they did.

Nowadays, things are quite different. The development of a modern bomber, for example, requires the efforts of hundreds of designers, mathematicians and engineers for several years, and complicated and expensive tools are required to build it.

So, when air forces or airlines want a new aeroplane, they usually prepare a list of all the things they want the aircraft to do. This list is called a specification and in the case of a bomber might be relatively simple, asking for a machine able to carry 10,000 lb. of bombs 8,000 miles. In the case of a new airliner it would probably specify such things as the number of passengers to be carried, the minimum range and cruising speed, maximum distances for landing and take-off, followed by pages of detail of radio, radar, and other equipment that must be provided.

Competition to build the new aeroplane will be keen, and the chief designer and his team at each of the aircraft companies eager to win the contract will vie with one another in attempting to pack the required payload and equipment into the smallest, cheapest and most efficient aeroplane possible.

Let us imagine the specification is for an airliner able to carry 80 passengers for 3,000

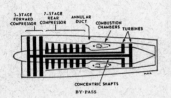

First problem confronting the aircraft designer is how to pack the required number of passengers, weight of fuel, baggage, radio and equipment into the smallest, most efficient airframe. Then he must decide what type of engine to use. Shall it be a turbo-prop or turbojet, straightforward axial-flow or by-pass . . . and so on.

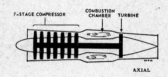

miles at 500 m.p.h. Obviously, only a big aircraft with powerful engines could do this, and the chief designer's first task is to decide what type of engine to use—turboprop or turbojet. If a turbojet seems suitable, should it be of the simple axial-flow or by-pass type? There is a big temptation to use well-proven engines free from "bugs". To do so, however, might make the aircraft out of date before it flew and so new and untried engines are usually chosen. The wing area of the new aeroplane will be largely governed by the loaded weight of the aircraft and its take-off and landing requirements, but the designer must choose between short stubby wings or long slender ones, or between a swept wing or delta wing. Having decided these and many other vital questions, the chief designer is able to make sketches of the sort of aeroplane he has in mind. The three pictures on the right show different airliner designs intended for much the same job.

The airline which prepared the specification carefully considers the various aircraft offered by the competing companies and then awards a contract for the one which it thinks is best for its particular needs.

As soon as the contract has been signed, the firm's Drawing Office is put to work. First of all, drawings are made showing the exact outside shape of the aircraft. These are used both for constructing the jigs on which the first aircraft will be made and special scale models for wind-tunnel tests to ensure that the aircraft is sound aerodynamically.

Readers of this book who have made flying model aircraft will know how modellers either add a piece of lead to the nose, or slide the wing along the fuselage if the plane does not fly properly. But this cannot be done on real aircraft; these have to be right from the start. By blowing air past a model in a wind tunnel and measuring the way it rises, falls or rolls sideways, aerodynamicists can tell exactly how the full-size aeroplane will fly.

This? . . .

. . . or this?

. . . or this?

As soon as the outside shape has been settled, draughtsmen start designing hundreds of ribs, spars, fuselage frames and a host of other components which make up the complete aircraft. Simultaneously, technicians in the Weights and Stress departments begin to calculate the weight and strength of every part. This is most important because if the aircraft is too heavy it might not, at the very worst, be able to take off—which has actually happened more than once. In any case, every unnecessary pound of structure weight will reduce the load it is able to carry. Yet, even a

The interior of the fuselage must next be fitted out. On the flight deck there is a maze of controls and instruments to install, like this engineer's panel which provides control of the fuel, cabin air-conditioning and electrical systems of the Comet 4. The passenger cabin must be furnished to the customer's individual whims, with different seating, colour schemes and equipment for every airline.

Time now to install the engines, and here we see one of the four 10,500-lb. thrust Rolls-Royce Avon turbojets about to be hoisted up into its wing-root housing. Ease of access for servicing and replacement is a primary requirement in an airliner, which must spend as much time as possible in the air if it is to make money. After the engines are in place, they will each be fitted with a noise suppressor.

(*Above*) Nearly complete. The top of the fuselage is painted white, to help keep the cabin cool while the aircraft is on the ground in tropical countries. The remainder is polished until it shines like a mirror. Finally comes the big day when the Comet is rolled out for the first time (*above right*). The pilot and his crew carefully check all controls, turn on to the runway and, after an incredibly short run, the airliner begins to climb steeply away (*right*).

The first Comet 4 flew on 27th April, 1958, and entered service with B.O.A.C. on 4th October, when it inaugurated the first scheduled jet airliner service across the Atlantic.

How an Aeroplane Works

BEFORE we can even begin to understand how an aeroplane works, we must first learn a little about the air in which all flying takes place. The air around us is merely the bottom of an immense atmospheric ocean which completely envelopes the earth. It is invisible and so thin that we are not normally aware of its existence. This makes it difficult for us to realise that like all other substances air has properties.

The most important fact to remember is that air has density. Any reader who can dive

WEIGHT OF ONE CUBIC FOOT OF AIR — ·08LB.

WEIGHT OF AIR IN AN ORDINARY ROOM — ABOUT 150LB.

WEIGHT OF COLUMN OF AIR PRESSING ON EVERY SQUARE FT. OF THE EARTH IS NEARLY A TON.

TOTAL WEIGHT OF AIR ON GT. BRITAIN IS ABOUT 2,500,000,000,000 TONS.

will probably have experienced the sensation of falling flat on to the surface of water—this indicates very forcefully that water has density and can thus exert forces which have to be treated carefully. Of course, the density of air is low compared with water, but parachutists who delay opening their 'chutes find it causes just such a jerk as is encountered when falling on to the surface of water.

You begin to realise—perhaps unknowingly—that air has density when riding a bicycle against a high wind. You get tired quickly because your muscles are working harder to overcome the considerable amount of extra resistance caused by the greater movement of the air past you.

Because it has density, air has weight—probably more than you think. For example, how much do you think the air in your dining-room weighs? 1 lb.? 10 lb.? Or 20 lb.? All these answers would be hopelessly wrong—it is nearer 150 lb.—or considerably more than a sack of coal!

It is the density of air that makes all flight possible. Balloons, kites, parachutes, gliders, swift fighters, ponderous freighters, sleek air-liners—all are supported in the air by forces which are entirely dependent on its density.

If we could "see" the air moving past an aeroplane it would make understanding how an aeroplane works much easier. Although this can be done to a certain extent by injecting smoke into special wind tunnels, this book explains it by means of the specially drawn pictures appearing on the following pages.

═══ D R A G ═══

Air is invisible, but that does not mean it is not there, or that it cannot exert considerable force. Think of the damage caused by a hurricane, which is only air in a hurry, and test the strength of air by putting your hand out of the window of a fast train, after making sure nothing is coming the other way.

FLAT PLATE DRAG

We can see water flowing round a ship. Air flows in a similar way, and, if we could see it, we should understand more easily how an aeroplane works.

We should, for example, be able to see that air flows round a flat plate like this ————————————————————————→

Because air does not flow smoothly round the plate, but swirls in all directions behind it, it creates what is called drag. Drag is the aircraft designer's public enemy No. 1, as its effect is like a brake holding back the aeroplane. Experiments have shown that for speeds between about 100 and 500 m.p.h., the drag of a body depends on four things—its shape, its frontal area, the square of its speed and the density of the air:

| SHAPE | FRONTAL AREA | THE SQUARE OF ITS SPEED | DENSITY OF THE AIR |

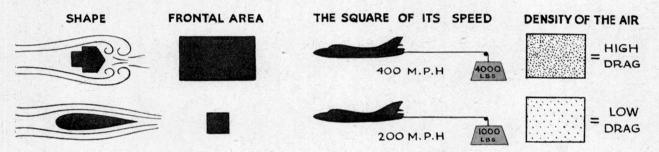

"Square of the speed" means that when the speed is doubled the drag is multiplied by four. Three times the speed would produce nine times the drag. Thus, if the drag of an aeroplane were 1,000 lb. at 200 m.p.h., it would be 4,000 lb. at 400 m.p.h., which is why a big increase in engine power is needed to give a relatively small increase in speed.

If the early pioneers could have seen air flowing past their aircraft while flying, they would have realised much sooner that they could reduce drag, and thus increase their speed, by "streamlining". The drag of a streamlined section, as shown in the diagram on the right, is only about $\frac{1}{20}$th of the drag of the flat plate shown above.

STREAMLINED DRAG

If designers had known this, retractable undercarriages would have been adopted earlier, and time and money would not have been wasted on machines like Phillips' "Venetian Blind" of 1907. It is so important to reduce drag that many modern aircraft are highly polished to make their skins really smooth—and designers are seriously concerned with the problem of stopping flies "landing" on aeroplane wings and spoiling the airflow.

Minute specks of dust or tiny insects can cause a wedge of disturbed air sufficient to slow down a jet plane by many m.p.h., as shown in the drawing on the right.

PHILLIPS'
'VENETIAN BLIND'

LIFT

A wing gets its "lift" in two ways. Air flowing over its deeply-curved top surface has to travel further to get from the leading edge to the trailing edge than air passing over its flatter under-surface. It therefore travels faster, and this lowers its pressure, creating suction. Three-quarters of the total lift is obtained this way. The other quarter comes from the air passing beneath the wing, which is slowed down and compressed by the wing, so that its pressure is increased and it pushes the wing upwards.

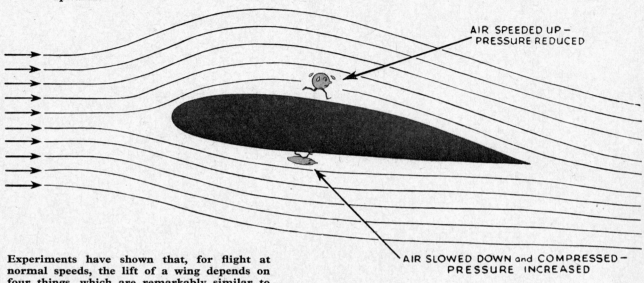

AIR SPEEDED UP—
PRESSURE REDUCED

AIR SLOWED DOWN and COMPRESSED—
PRESSURE INCREASED

Experiments have shown that, for flight at normal speeds, the lift of a wing depends on four things, which are remarkably similar to those which govern drag. They are its section, its area, the square of the speed, and the density of the air.

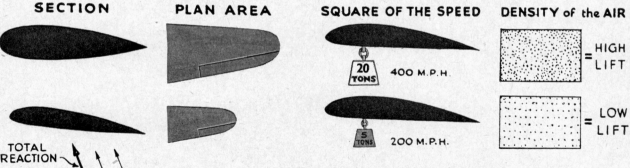

SECTION   **PLAN AREA**   **SQUARE OF THE SPEED**   **DENSITY of the AIR**

20 TONS   400 M.P.H.

= HIGH LIFT

5 TONS   200 M.P.H.

= LOW LIFT

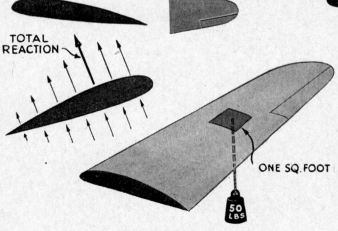

TOTAL REACTION

ONE SQ. FOOT

50 LBS

If we add together the suction above the wing and the upward force exerted by the air underneath it, we get what is called the "total reaction". This is smaller than one would expect, being usually less than ½ lb. for every sq. in. at normal speeds, so that every sq. ft. of the wing gives a lift of about 50 lb. A wing area of 300 sq. ft. is thus needed to lift an aeroplane weighing 15,000 lb.—the weight of a small fighter plane—at comparatively low speeds.

LIFT (Continued)

The angle at which a wing meets oncoming airflow in flight is called the angle of attack, and this is shown in this diagram. This angle is important, as the bigger it is the more the wing will push down and compress the airflow underneath it, so increasing the pressure under the wing, and, hence, the lift. Unfortunately, it also increases the drag, so there is a limit to its usefulness.

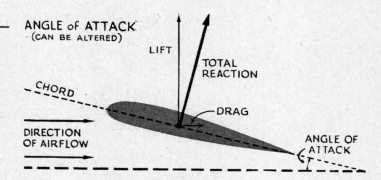

Angle of attack should not be confused with the angle of incidence, which is the angle at which the wing is set in relation to the fuselage. The angle of attack varies as an aircraft climbs or dives; the angle of incidence remains the same.

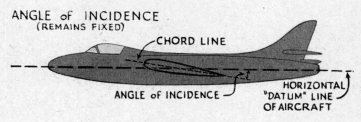

At first, as the angle of attack of a wing is increased its lift goes up faster than the drag, until at an angle of 4 degrees it may be as much as 12 times as great. But as the angle of attack is made bigger still, drag begins to increase faster than the lift, until a point is reached, where, instead of increasing the lift begins to fall rapidly.

This occurs at an angle of about 15 degrees, and what happens is shown in this diagram. The wing is inclined so steeply that the effect of its streamlined shape is lost—air no longer flows smoothly over its top surface, and the suction, which is responsible for about three-quarters of the total lift, disappears.

The wing is said to be stalled.

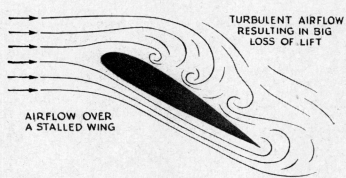

TURBULENT AIRFLOW RESULTING IN BIG LOSS OF LIFT

AIRFLOW OVER A STALLED WING

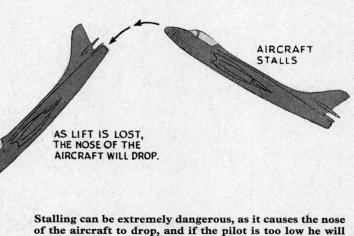

AIRCRAFT STALLS

AS LIFT IS LOST, THE NOSE OF THE AIRCRAFT WILL DROP.

THE ANGLE OF ATTACK WILL BE REDUCED, AND THE LIFT REGAINED

Stalling can be extremely dangerous, as it causes the nose of the aircraft to drop, and if the pilot is too low he will crash.

At high altitudes it is not so serious, because as the aircraft falls the angle of attack is reduced and the lift regained, so that the pilot is able to regain control.

─SLOTS─

Ability to land slowly and fly slowly without stalling is one of the biggest safety features any aeroplane can have. Slow flying is also an essential requirement for aircraft used in military observation, crop spraying and similar duties.

Unfortunately, the slower an aeroplane flies, the greater becomes the angle of attack of its wing, and, unless the pilot is careful, it can easily be stalled.

Designers have gone to great lengths to try and prevent, or at least delay, the break-up of smooth airflow over the wing at high angles of attack, to remove the danger of stalling. Best-known and most successful anti-stall device is the wing leading-edge slot.

The slot was invented in 1919 by the British Handley Page Company, whose designer discovered that if a small additional "wing" or slat were placed in front of the main wing, it would prevent the latter stalling at angles of attack up to at least 25 degrees, and also double its lift. The reason for this is shown on the right.

Handley Page slots soon proved their value, and in 1928 the Air Ministry ordered that they should be fitted to all British service aircraft. Accidents to R.A.F. warplanes at once dropped from 54 in the year before slots were fitted to 31, and, since then, hundreds of different types of aircraft, from 43 countries have been fitted with Handley Page slots.

The diagram on the right shows how a slot works. By splitting the air-flow at the wing leading-edge, the slot reduces the pressure of the air, so that it flows smoothly back over the entire top surface of the wing, even at high angles of attack.

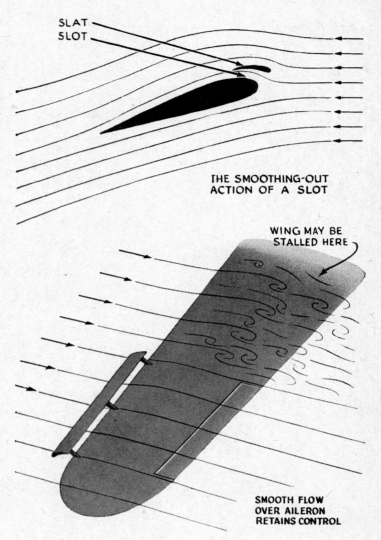

SLAT
SLOT

THE SMOOTHING-OUT
ACTION OF A SLOT

WING MAY BE
STALLED HERE

SMOOTH FLOW
OVER AILERON
RETAINS CONTROL

The leading-edge slats can be seen clearly on this Scottish Aviation Prestwick Pioneer STOL aircraft. Together with the large Fowler flaps, they enable the Pioneer to operate into and out of restricted spaces, making it particularly suitable for operations in jungle areas like Malaya. Even when there is no wind to help, it will take off in only 240 ft. and land in 200 ft., carrying a full load.

-VARIABLE INCIDENCE -

Unfortunately, it is not practicable to make full use of the increased lift offered by slots, as maximum lift is obtained at an angle of attack of 25 degrees. If the wing of an average airliner were set at such an angle to the airflow, its fuselage would be tilted to a most uncomfortable attitude, and the pilot would probably be unable to see past the aircraft's nose!

In any case, much of the increased lift produced by the slots would be cancelled out by the extra weight of the stalky undercarriage that would have to be fitted.

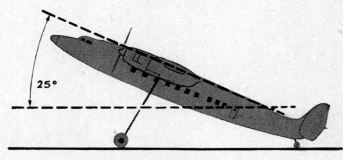

The stalky undercarriage problem could be overcome by setting the wing at a large angle of incidence. But this would be even worse for the passengers, as the best angle of attack for normal cruising flight is about 4 degrees, and the airliner would fly something like this.

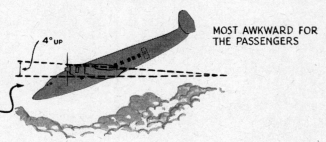

MOST AWKWARD FOR THE PASSENGERS

A more practical idea is to have what is called a variable incidence wing, so that the angle of incidence can be increased to ensure good lift and low speeds for take-off and landing, and reduced for normal cruising flight.

This is not only complicated, but also very expensive. So variable incidence wings can only be considered for use on specialised types of aircraft where an unusually low landing speed and fairly high cruising speed are of the utmost importance.

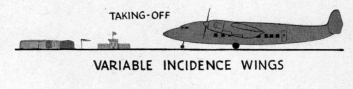

TAKING-OFF

VARIABLE INCIDENCE WINGS

IN FLIGHT

The Chance Vought F8U Crusader naval fighter is one of the few aeroplanes to have a variable-incidence wing. When raised, as shown here, and with both leading and trailing-edge flaps drooped to increase the wing camber, the Crusader becomes airborne much more quickly than would otherwise be the case. Similarly, it is able to land under control at much lower speeds, with the fuselage horizontal to give the pilot a good forward view for deck-landing.

FLAPS

THE SIMPLE FLAP CAN INCREASE
THE LIFT OF A WING BY AS MUCH
AS A HALF

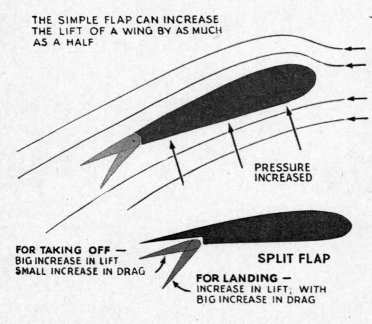

PRESSURE
INCREASED

FOR TAKING OFF —
BIG INCREASE IN LIFT
SMALL INCREASE IN DRAG

SPLIT FLAP

FOR LANDING —
INCREASE IN LIFT, WITH
BIG INCREASE IN DRAG

FOWLER FLAP

AUXILIARY
AEROFOIL
FLAPS

TAKE-OFF

CRUISING

LANDING

Fortunately, designers can ensure low landing speeds for fast aeroplanes by using another invention—flaps. These are an essential aid to safe flying for modern aircraft, as they not only increase the lift of a wing when necessary, but also increase the drag when required, to give slower landing speeds. As they add little to the drag of a wing when retracted in flight, they can be fitted quite happily to even the fastest aircraft.

The main advantage of using flaps rather than slots is that they increase lift without much increase in the angle of attack, so the aircraft does not have to fly with its nose stuck up in the air.

The simple type of flap can increase the lift of a wing by as much as 50%.

The split flap increases lift by as much as 70%. An added advantage is that the top surface of the wing is unbroken by a hinge line.

The Fowler flap, by providing at the same time a virtual increase in wing area and camber, almost doubles the lift of a wing without altering its angle of attack. It is often used on flying-boats and airliners.

As their name implies, auxiliary aerofoil flaps are like miniature wings mounted behind and slightly below the main wings. They are carried on a link mechanism, so that they can be fully retracted and therefore offer little drag for high-speed flight. When extended for cruising, they almost turn a monoplane into a biplane, doubling lift in some cases. For landing, they move aft to act as Fowler-type flaps.

Two large plain flaps and two split flaps under each wing give the Comet 4 an exceptionally low landing speed.

— STABILITY —

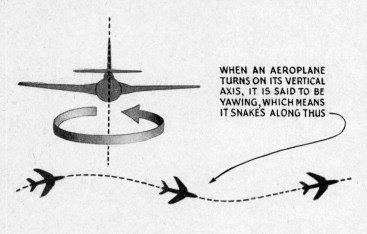

WHEN AN AEROPLANE TURNS ON ITS VERTICAL AXIS, IT IS SAID TO BE YAWING, WHICH MEANS IT SNAKES ALONG THUS

Stability is just about the most important feature of any aeroplane, for, if it is very unstable, it may be difficult to fly, or even may not leave the ground at all.

It is quite easy to explain stability, as it applies to bicycles as much as to aeroplanes. A bicycle is, in fact, very unstable sideways—whilst stationary it is impossible to sit on one and not fall over.

A tricycle, on the other hand, is very stable. It can be rocked sideways fairly violently without falling over, and will quickly right itself afterwards.

In the same way, a stable aeroplane, if it is jerked or rocked by a gust of wind, or deflected from its path in some way or other, will return to straight and level flight without any action on the part of its pilot.

As aeroplanes move in all three dimensions, designers have to make sure that their aircraft are stable in all directions. There are three ways in which an aeroplane can move, or rotate, and it does so about three different axes, all of which pass through its centre of gravity (the point about which it is perfectly balanced). The diagrams on the left should help you to understand this better.

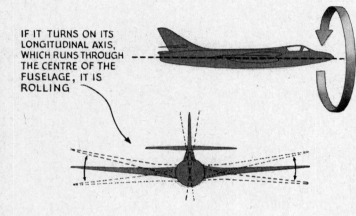

IF IT TURNS ON ITS LONGITUDINAL AXIS, WHICH RUNS THROUGH THE CENTRE OF THE FUSELAGE, IT IS ROLLING

To be stable, an aeroplane must be so designed that when it is rocked by a gust of wind about any of its three axes, it will return to normal straight and level flight without any action on the part of its pilot.

This is done as follows:

Pitching is dealt with by the tailplane. If an aeroplane begins to pitch so that its tail drops, the tail is pushed up again immediately by the force of the airflow under the tailplane.

Similarly, if the nose drops, a downward force on the top of the tailplane pushes it downwards and the aircraft resumes an even keel.

Lateral, or sideways stability, is achieved by "bending the wings up" to give them what is called a dihedral angle. This is easy enough, but it is not so easy to understand how it stops an aeroplane rolling after a gust of wind has tilted it sideways. What happens is this:

The aircraft, having been struck by a gust of wind, starts to roll, and before it can be righted, the

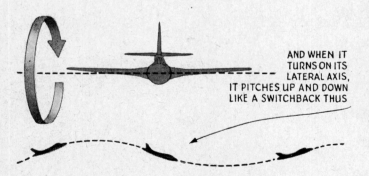

AND WHEN IT TURNS ON ITS LATERAL AXIS, IT PITCHES UP AND DOWN LIKE A SWITCHBACK THUS

HOW TAILPLANE CORRECTS PITCHING

LIFT FROM WING

CENTRE OF GRAVITY, ABOUT WHICH AEROPLANE ROTATES.

AIRFLOW ACTS ON TAILPLANE, AND UPWARD FORCE TENDS TO LIFT THE TAIL AND RETURN AIRCRAFT TO LEVEL FLIGHT.

roll must be checked. This is ensured by the ordinary law of lift, thus—the rising wing is moving away from the air, so its lift is reduced. The dropping wing, on the other side, is meeting the air, however, and its lift is increased. This stops the aircraft rolling farther, but it is still flying with its wing well down, and this upsets the usual balance of lift and weight, so that it begins to slide sideways in what is called a sideslip.

This is where the dihedral angle really comes in. As the aeroplane slides sideways, airflow from the side pushes up under the lower wing, increasing its lift, and the aircraft is soon levelled out again.

Easiest to understand, but often the most difficult to achieve, is directional stability—sometimes called weathercock stability, as an aeroplane obtains it in the same way as a weathercock.

The centre of gravity in an aeroplane corresponds with the pivot of the weathercock, which allows the arrow to turn round horizontally. The tail of a weathercock is made big enough to ensure that the arrow will always point into the wind: in the same way, the fin area of an aeroplane must be sufficiently large to ensure that, if the 'plane begins to yaw, it will always turn back into the wind. The length of fuselage makes a difference to the fin area. A short fuselage needs a large fin area to give it sufficient leverage; a smaller fin is quite sufficient for an aircraft with a long fuselage.

A high degree of stability, as we have seen, is essential for safe flight. But designers must avoid making their aircraft too stable, because a pilot cannot begin to manœuvre his aeroplane in any direction until he has overcome its inherent stability.

The way he overcomes it is described on the next two pages.

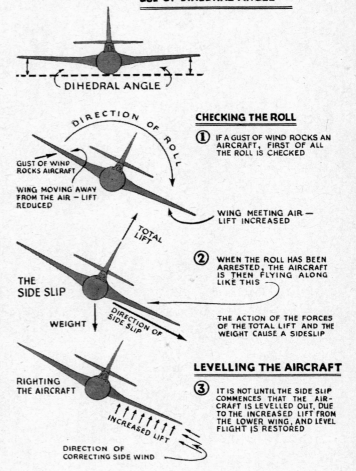

DIHEDRAL ANGLE

CHECKING THE ROLL

① IF A GUST OF WIND ROCKS AN AIRCRAFT, FIRST OF ALL THE ROLL IS CHECKED

DIRECTION OF ROLL

GUST OF WIND ROCKS AIRCRAFT

WING MOVING AWAY FROM THE AIR – LIFT REDUCED

WING MEETING AIR — LIFT INCREASED

② WHEN THE ROLL HAS BEEN ARRESTED, THE AIRCRAFT IS THEN FLYING ALONG LIKE THIS

THE ACTION OF THE FORCES OF THE TOTAL LIFT AND THE WEIGHT CAUSE A SIDESLIP

TOTAL LIFT

THE SIDE SLIP

WEIGHT

DIRECTION OF SIDE SLIP

LEVELLING THE AIRCRAFT

③ IT IS NOT UNTIL THE SIDE SLIP COMMENCES THAT THE AIRCRAFT IS LEVELLED OUT, DUE TO THE INCREASED LIFT FROM THE LOWER WING, AND LEVEL FLIGHT IS RESTORED

RIGHTING THE AIRCRAFT

INCREASED LIFT

DIRECTION OF CORRECTING SIDE WIND

DIRECTIONAL STABILITY

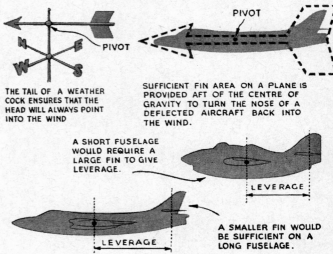

PIVOT

PIVOT

THE TAIL OF A WEATHER COCK ENSURES THAT THE HEAD WILL ALWAYS POINT INTO THE WIND

SUFFICIENT FIN AREA ON A PLANE IS PROVIDED AFT OF THE CENTRE OF GRAVITY TO TURN THE NOSE OF A DEFLECTED AIRCRAFT BACK INTO THE WIND.

A SHORT FUSELAGE WOULD REQUIRE A LARGE FIN TO GIVE LEVERAGE.

LEVERAGE

A SMALLER FIN WOULD BE SUFFICIENT ON A LONG FUSELAGE.

LEVERAGE

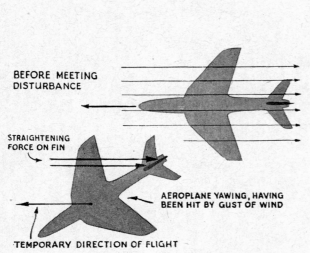

BEFORE MEETING DISTURBANCE

STRAIGHTENING FORCE ON FIN

AEROPLANE YAWING, HAVING BEEN HIT BY GUST OF WIND

TEMPORARY DIRECTION OF FLIGHT

FLYING CONTROL SURFACES

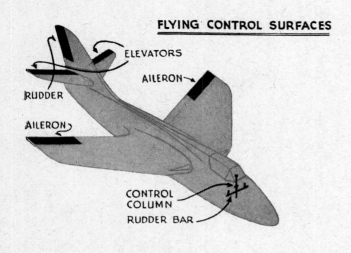

ELEVATORS

AILERON

RUDDER

AILERON

CONTROL COLUMN

RUDDER BAR

— CONTROLS —

The pilot controls his direction of flight by moving the rudder, the ailerons and the elevators of his aeroplane.

The rudder is usually moved by means of a foot-operated rudder bar; the ailerons are operated by a side-to-side movement of the control column (or joystick), which also, by a backward and forward action, operates the elevators.

All these control surfaces work on the same principle. Expressed in simple terms, air prefers to travel in straight lines, consequently, when a control surface is moved, as shown in the diagram below, the air which is deflected is also compressed, which builds up a pressure.

This pressure pushes against the control surface, and tries to straighten it out, so that the air will flow smoothly again. This tends to move the whole aeroplane in the opposite direction.

So, by moving the correct controls, the pilot can manœuvre his aircraft in any direction. For example, if the rudder bar is pushed forward with the right foot, the rudder will move to the right. The airflow reacts by pushing the tail to the left, and the aircraft begins to turn to the right, about its vertical axis. Using the rudder alone, however, would produce a flat turn and the aeroplane would begin side-slipping to the left. So the pilot also banks his aeroplane slightly, just as a motor cyclist leans over when going round a corner, by moving his control column to the right. Thus, both ailerons and rudder are usually used for turning.

Similarly, pulling the control column backward raises the elevators, and the aircraft climbs. When it is pushed forward, the aircraft dives.

THE RUDDER BAR OPERATES THE RUDDER

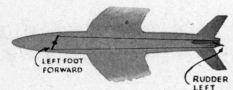

LEFT FOOT FORWARD

RUDDER LEFT

THE CONTROL COLUMN

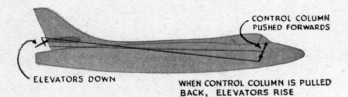

CONTROL COLUMN PUSHED FORWARDS

ELEVATORS DOWN

WHEN CONTROL COLUMN IS PULLED BACK, ELEVATORS RISE

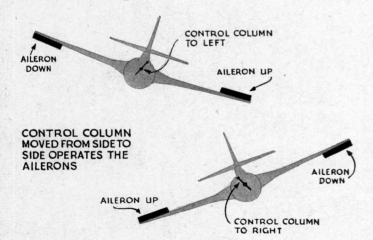

CONTROL COLUMN TO LEFT

AILERON DOWN

AILERON UP

CONTROL COLUMN MOVED FROM SIDE TO SIDE OPERATES THE AILERONS

AILERON UP

AILERON DOWN

CONTROL COLUMN TO RIGHT

PRINCIPLE OF CONTROL SURFACES

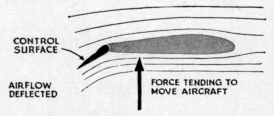

CONTROL SURFACE

AIRFLOW DEFLECTED

FORCE TENDING TO MOVE AIRCRAFT

Control surfaces all work on the same principle. When they are moved, the air is deflected, and a force is created, tending to move the aircraft.

125

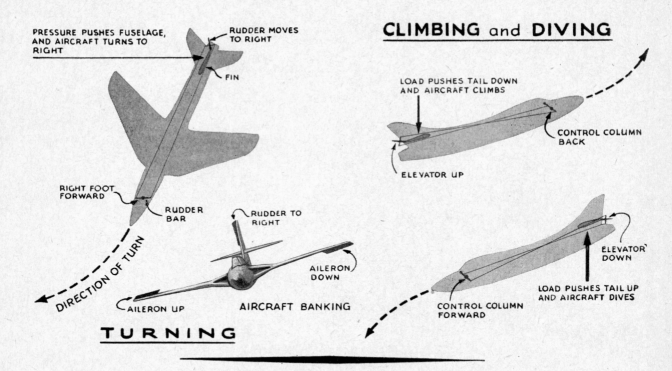

PRESSURE PUSHES FUSELAGE, AND AIRCRAFT TURNS TO RIGHT

RUDDER MOVES TO RIGHT

FIN

RIGHT FOOT FORWARD

RUDDER BAR

RUDDER TO RIGHT

AILERON DOWN

AILERON UP

DIRECTION OF TURN

AIRCRAFT BANKING

TURNING

CLIMBING and DIVING

LOAD PUSHES TAIL DOWN AND AIRCRAFT CLIMBS

CONTROL COLUMN BACK

ELEVATOR UP

ELEVATOR DOWN

LOAD PUSHES TAIL UP AND AIRCRAFT DIVES

CONTROL COLUMN FORWARD

SUPERSONICS

So far, we have considered only how aeroplanes work at speeds up to about 500 m.p.h. Above this speed important changes take place.

As an aeroplane approaches the speed at which sound travels through the air—about 760 m.p.h. at sea level, falling to about 660 m.p.h. at heights above 36,000 ft.—the air no longer flows smoothly over the wing as described earlier. Sudden changes take place in density and pressure of the air flowing past the wing, with accompanying drastic increases in drag and a decrease in lift. Instead of being divided smoothly, the air is compressed by the wing, "shock waves" are formed, and a very big expenditure of power is necessary to increase speed even by a small amount. The force that can be exerted by the compressed air (or compressibility) shock waves is so great that unless high-speed aircraft are specially designed, they could be smashed to pieces in a few seconds.

Because of these terrific forces, it is vital for a pilot to know when he is flying near the speed of sound.

He cannot just look at the air-speed indicator because, as explained above, the speed of sound varies by over 100 m.p.h. at different heights.

An aeroplane may be safe flying at 9/10ths the speed of sound—that is 680 m.p.h. at sea level. But if it tried to reach this speed at 36,000 ft. it would be flying 20 m.p.h. *faster* than the speed of sound—and would probably wreck itself.

So instead of measuring speed in miles per hour, the term "Mach number" is used, and this is simply the relationship between the actual speed of the aircraft and the speed of sound at the height at which it is flying. Thus a speed of Mach 2·0 means twice the speed of sound or 1,520 m.p.h. at sea level, and Mach 0·5 is equivalent to 380 m.p.h. at sea level, or 330 m.p.h. at 36,000 ft.

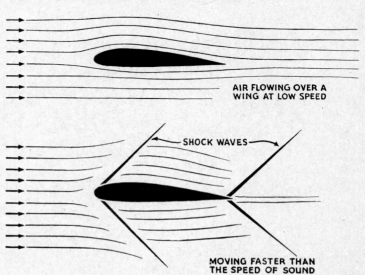

AIR FLOWING OVER A WING AT LOW SPEED

SHOCK WAVES

MOVING FASTER THAN THE SPEED OF SOUND

DEVELOPMENT OF A THEME ──

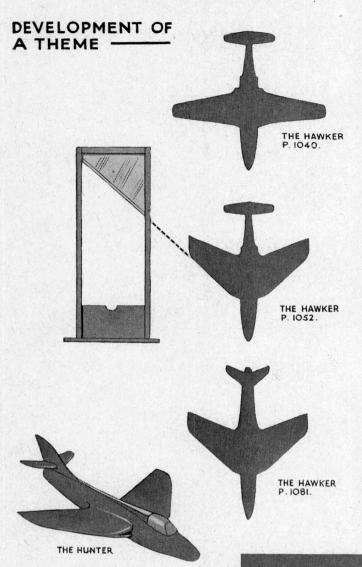

THE HAWKER
P. 1040.

THE HAWKER
P. 1052.

THE HAWKER
P. 1081.

THE HUNTER

A major problem facing designers of high speed aircraft is to postpone the build-up of the compressibility shock waves for as long as possible, and the most usual solution is to sweep back the wings. It is difficult to explain just why sweptback wings should do this. Very simply it can be said that they have a "smoothing" effect on the airflow and cut through it more smoothly, in much the same way that a guillotine is more efficient if the blade is set at an angle!

It is interesting to trace the development of the Hawker jet 'planes which have led up to the Hunter fighter.

The first was the straight-winged P.1040. This was followed by the P.1052, on which the wings were swept in order to gain a few extra precious miles per hour. The tailplane and fin followed suit on the P.1081, which had also a redesigned fuselage with the jet exhausting at the tail instead of at the wing roots as on the P.1040 and P.1052. More sharply swept wings and streamlined fuselage housing a more powerful engine ensure an even higher maximum speed for the Hunter.

Many experts consider that the best way to achieve still higher performance is to build aircraft with "delta" wings, so-called because of their resemblance to the Greek letter Δ (Delta). The result looks remarkably similar to a schoolboy's paper dart.

In addition to being highly sweptback, with a low wing loading and small span in relation to its length, the delta has several other advantages. For example it is very stiff and strong, there is plenty of room inside it for engines, undercarriage, fuel and equipment; and, most important of all, it offers improved controllability for flight at and beyond the speed of sound.

Typical of the many fine delta-wing aeroplanes built in recent years is the Fairey Delta 2 research aircraft, in which test pilot Peter Twiss set up a world speed record of 1,132 m.p.h. in March 1956. It was the first official "over-1,000 m.p.h." record.

AREA RULE

In these days of thin wings and ever finer streamlining, the appearance of various aircraft with odd-looking, pinched-in, fuselages has come as a surprise. Even more bewildering are the aircraft on which bulges have been added to what appeared to be a perfectly streamlined fuselage.

The reason for this is that at very high speeds the shape of an aircraft as a whole has to be considered and not the shape of the fuselage, wings and tail unit by themselves. Thus, a fuselage which may be quite satisfactory by itself, may become the wrong shape when the wings are attached. To ensure that the shape is satisfactory, the Area Rule has to be applied.

If we slice through the aircraft at different points as shown on the adjacent diagram, it is obvious that the area is much greater where the wings meet the fuselage. As a result the *total* cross-sectional area may continue to increase to a point well back from the nose, when it should be thinning down to give the familiar streamlined "wing" shape. This thinning can be achieved by "waisting" the

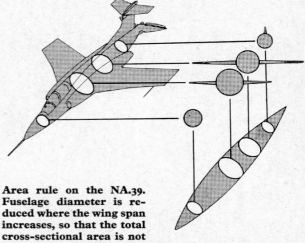

Area rule on the NA.39. Fuselage diameter is reduced where the wing span increases, so that the total cross-sectional area is not more than that of ideal streamline shape at the same relative position.

fuselage where the wing is providing too much of the total cross-sectional area. Sometimes, at the extreme tail, the wing and fuselage taper off too sharply to provide the desired shape. In this case the rear of the fuselage can be fattened to ensure that it complies with the area rule.

The familiar "coke-bottle" shape of an area-ruled fuselage is plainly evident in this view of the Blackburn NA.39. Also shown in this picture, and in the diagram above, are the sideways-opening air-brakes at the tail, formed by splitting the fuselage tail-cone.

How a Helicopter Works

A HELICOPTER is basically an aeroplane on which the conventional fixed wing is replaced by a moving wing, called a rotor.

The previous section titled "How an Aeroplane Works" describes how air flowing past a wing generates lift. On an ordinary aeroplane the flow of air is obtained by the whole

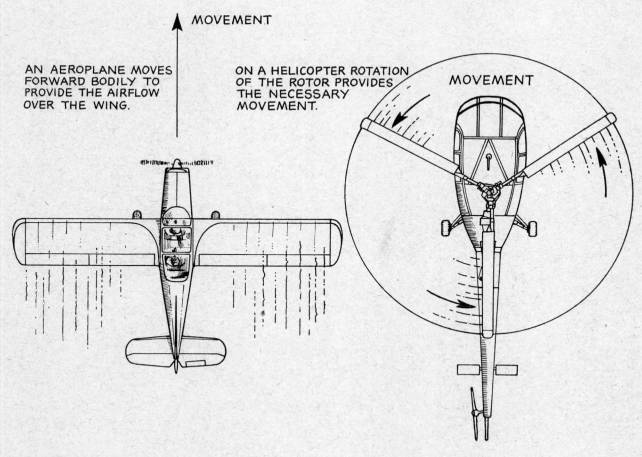

MOVEMENT

AN AEROPLANE MOVES FORWARD BODILY TO PROVIDE THE AIRFLOW OVER THE WING.

ON A HELICOPTER ROTATION OF THE ROTOR PROVIDES THE NECESSARY MOVEMENT.

MOVEMENT

aircraft moving through the air. A helicopter however, obtains its lift by spinning its rotor. Thus, a helicopter need not move bodily to obtain lift as does a conventional aeroplane. Because of this a helicopter can rise and descend vertically and hover, apparently motionless, in the sky. We say "apparently" motionless, because all the time, of course, the rotor will be spinning round to provide the flow of air over the blades to generate the desired lift.

To be useful, a helicopter has to be able to fly forward as well as hover, and the force required to pull the machine along is obtained not from a separate propeller at the front, but from the main rotor itself. This is obtained by tilting the whole rotor in the direction it is required to go so that the total rotor lift provides both the vertical lift supporting the machine and the horizontal force required to pull it along.

Basically, then, the helicopter idea is quite simple, but unfortunately in practice it becomes very complicated. For example, you will know that if a propeller is turned in one direction there is a torque reaction in the

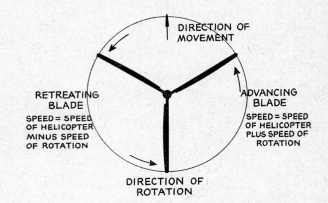

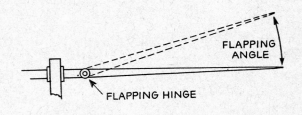

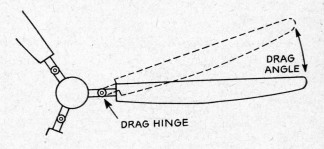

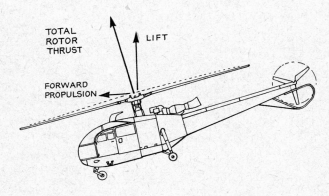

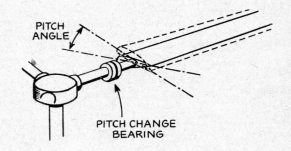

THE THREE HINGES REQUIRED ON A HELICOPTER BLADE

opposite direction. If a helicopter only had its main rotor, the fuselage would start spinning in the opposite direction to the rotor. To counteract this torque a vertical tail rotor is normally used to exert a side thrust in the required direction.

130

The construction of the main rotor is also much more complicated than it appears to be at first sight. If you look at the accompanying diagram it will be seen that when a helicopter is travelling forward the rotor blades pass through the air at different speeds. When "advancing" a blade has a speed equal to its own speed of rotation plus the speed of the helicopter's movement, while the speed of the "retreating" blade is equal to the speed of rotation minus the speed of movement. This creates more lift on one side than the other which, if not allowed for, would turn the helicopter over—as sometimes happened in the early days! To prevent this, the blades are attached to the rotor head by a "flapping" hinge. This allows the blades to rise as they gain lift on the advancing side and fall as they lose lift on the retreating side, thus equalising the lift on both sides of the rotor.

Further complication arises from the fact that the advancing blades tend to speed up, and the retreating blades tend to slow down. This causes the blades to bend, which is obviously undesirable, and to prevent this a "drag" hinge is introduced, to allow the blades a limited degree of fore and aft movement.

All this allows the rotor to spin smoothly, but it would not enable us to get anywhere. Although the amount of lift being generated could be controlled by altering the speed of the rotor, this would impose heavy strains on the engine and be uneconomical in fuel. The better method is to alter the pitch of the rotor blades so that they develop more or less lift as required. This requires yet another hinge, which is called the "pitch change" bearing.

To control the helicopter by this method it has to be possible to vary the pitch angle of the blades as they rotate. This is not a simple thing to do mechanically, and is usually achieved through what is called a swashplate. This consists of two plates round the rotor shaft, the top one revolving with the rotor and the lower one being fixed to the fuselage.

Rods connect the upper plate to each of the rotor blades, so that when the swashplate is lifted up bodily the pitch of all the blades is increased equally; this is called "collective-pitch" change. By tilting the swashplate forward, the connecting rods reduce the pitch on the blades at the front and increase it at the rear. This is known as cyclic-pitch change, because as the blades revolve their pitch is continually changing—maximum pitch and most lift at the rear and smallest pitch and minimum lift at the front. This creates unequal loads, the effect of which is to tilt the whole rotor and cause the helicopter to move forward.

Two levers in the cockpit control the swash-plate; the collective-pitch lever raises and lowers it bodily; the control column controls the angle of the swashplate. As the helicopter flies in the direction the swashplate is tilted, backwards and sideways flight is possible as well as forward movement—adding to the versatility and usefulness of this type of machine.

Other mechanical complexities come into the picture and to deal with these thoroughly would make this introduction to how a helicopter works far too complicated.

Finally, do not confuse helicopters with Autogiros. The essential difference is that on Autogiros the rotor is unpowered, and a conventional propeller in the nose of the fuselage pulls the machine along, this action causing the rotor to spin automatically like the sails of a windmill.

*

How a Jet Engine Works

IN order to learn how a jet engine works we must first understand Sir Isaac Newton's Third Law of Motion which is: "To each and every action there is an equal and opposite reaction."

Written like that it looks rather frightening, but it is only the scientific way of explaining everyday facts such as why a boat moves away from the bank as you step ashore, or why a gun recoils when it is fired.

A jet engine throws a column of air backwards at high speed—that's the action. The reaction—equal and opposite—pushes the engine forward. It is important to realise that it is *not* pushed along by the pressure of its exhaust gases against the air behind it. If this were so, there would be no satellites or space travel with the type of rocket engine we know today, because in space there is no air for the exhaust to push against.

The following simple explanation of reaction may help you to understand exactly what happens. Imagine a firework "banger" inside an empty tin, closed at one end, as shown in the illustration. Now imagine the firework explodes and breaks into two pieces. One piece flies out of the end of the tin and obviously has no effect on it. The other piece, however, hits the closed end of the tin and moves the whole thing along.

A jet-engine is basically a more elaborate tin, in which the single explosion of the firework is replaced by a continuous explosion caused by the combustion of a mixture of air and fuel. All a jet-engine does is to compress air and mix it with fuel sprayed into the combustion chambers to cause the explosion. A great deal of power is needed to compress the air, and if an ordinary piston engine were used for this purpose it would be a very heavy and bulky unit. On the modern jet-engine the power is provided in a most ingenious manner. The exhaust gases rushing out of the rear of the engine are guided past a bladed wheel, called a turbine, causing it to rotate. But—and here's the clever part—the turbine is fixed to a shaft which in turn is fixed to the compressor. So, when the turbine rotates, the compressor rotates also. This is the basic

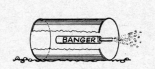

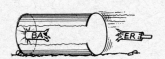

In this diagram the burning of fuel inside a jet-engine is symbolised by an exploding firework in an empty tin. The tin is pushed along not by the piece that flies out of the open end (the exhaust gases) but by the piece that hits the front (the reaction).

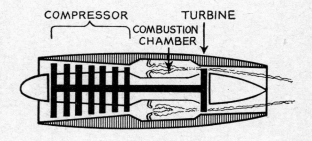

The basic simplicity of the turbojet is evident from this sectioned view. Note that there is only one moving part—the shaft to which the compressor and turbine are fixed.

simplicity of the jet-engine—not only does it develop tremendous power, it does so with the minimum of moving parts.

The turbine, in addition to turning the compressor, can be harnessed to drive a propeller, the engine then being known as a turboprop. Turboprops lose some of the high-speed performance qualities of the "pure" jet, but in exchange for speed the engines use much less fuel, and are more efficient at slow speeds. In the simplest turboprops the turbine shaft is extended forward of the compressor into a reduction gearing from which the propeller is driven.

To meet the demand for ever lower fuel consumption and ever higher thrust—now approaching the 30,000-lb. mark—complications have also been introduced into the basic simplicity of the turbojet engine. The easiest way to get more power is to add more stages to the compressor; but there comes a point where doing this causes uneven flow through the engine under certain airflow conditions. To overcome this the two-spool engine was developed. In this there are two turbines, each driving a separate compressor. The front compressor is known as the low-pressure compressor, and that behind it the high-pressure compressor. They are driven by the low-pressure turbine and the high-pressure turbine respectively.

In this form of engine there is no mechanical connection between the LP and HP

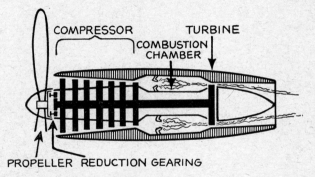

TURBOPROP. The shaft is extended forward of the compressor to drive a propeller.

systems, so that each can be operated at its best efficiency.

Turbojets burn fuel at a high rate and attempts are being made to overcome this by the development of the by-pass or fan engine. As can be seen from the illustration a by-pass engine is simply one in which some of the compressor blades are extended to become in effect low-diameter propellers. This arrangement has several advantages. First, the engine throws back a large column of air in addition to the central core of high-speed exhaust; this brings with it some of the higher efficiency of the propeller, and reduces fuel consumption. Secondly, the mass of air flowing round the outside of the engine cools it, and, not least important, the "tube" of cool air tends to damp down the harsh roar of the hot inner exhaust and this makes the engine quieter.

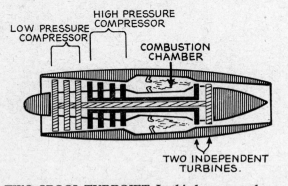

TWO-SPOOL TURBOJET. In this layout, used on the more powerful turbojets, separate compressors are driven by their own turbines.

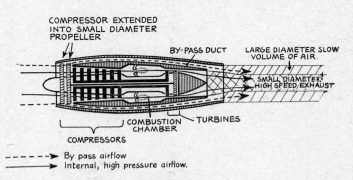

BY-PASS TURBOJET. In this, part of the compressor is extended to form a small propeller or fan, the air from which by-passes the combustion chamber and turbine.

STARFIGHTER PILOT

In the days of the old West made famous by TV films, the young men of America wore guns, spurs and rode horses. Today they wear pressure-suits and have swopped their tough swift horses for faster, stronger aircraft. Only the spurs remain. This is a typical day in the life of a pilot of one of the U.S.A.F.'s 1,400 m.p.h. Starfighters.

Up early, Capt. Robert Rayford has breakfast with his wife and son.

Arriving at the base, he collects his pressure-suit from a special room kept at constant temperature.

At the briefing, the purpose of the high-altitude and high-speed mission is explained.

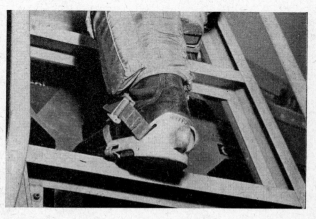

Climbing aboard. Note the "spurs" which lock the pilot's feet to the seat in an emergency ejection.

The controls of the supersonic fighter are given a thorough pre-flight check.

In the cockpit, Capt. Rayford checks his personal equipment with the help of a ground crew member.

Within seconds the Starfighter is airborne and able to climb faster than sound. Note the two deadly Sidewinder missiles, one on each wing tip. These seek out the target and home on to the heat radiation emitted by its jet exhaust. Sometimes Starfighters are "scrambled" to intercept approaching unidentified aircraft. This time, however, it is only a practice mission.

Back from the flight, Capt. Rayford signs the "supersonic" flight log.

Films taken during the mission are screened in the Squadron's projection room. Valuable lessons are learned in this manner, enabling improved techniques to be worked out.

Wings of War

IF what we read in some newspapers in 1957 had been true, this part of the aviation story would now consist of nothing but history. Guided missiles were becoming so formidable by then that the British Govern-ment took the bold step of planning the complete reorganisation of its armed forces. In the case of the R.A.F., there were to be no more piloted interceptor fighters after the supersonic Lightning, which was then entering

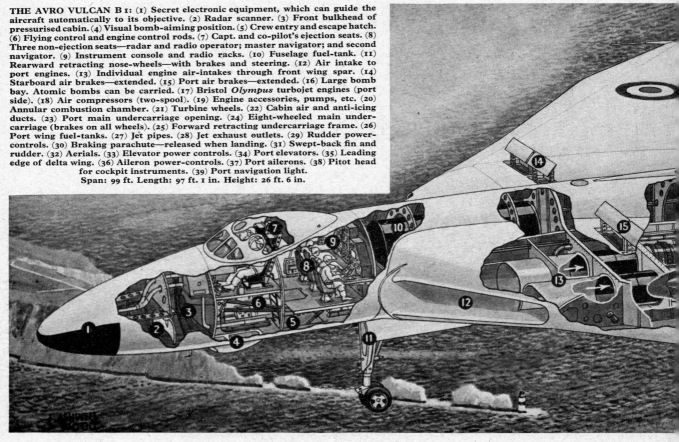

THE AVRO VULCAN B 1: (1) Secret electronic equipment, which can guide the aircraft automatically to its objective. (2) Radar scanner. (3) Front bulkhead of pressurised cabin. (4) Visual bomb-aiming position. (5) Crew entry and escape hatch. (6) Flying control and engine control rods. (7) Capt. and co-pilot's ejection seats. (8) Three non-ejection seats—radar and radio operator; master navigator; and second navigator. (9) Instrument console and radio racks. (10) Fuselage fuel-tank. (11) Rearward retracting nose-wheels—with brakes and steering. (12) Air intake to port engines. (13) Individual engine air-intakes through front wing spar. (14) Starboard air brakes—extended. (15) Port air brakes—extended. (16) Large bomb bay. Atomic bombs can be carried. (17) Bristol *Olympus* turbojet engines (port side). (18) Air compressors (two-spool). (19) Engine accessories, pumps, etc. (20) Annular combustion chamber. (21) Turbine wheels. (22) Cabin air and anti-icing ducts. (23) Port main undercarriage opening. (24) Eight-wheeled main under-carriage (brakes on all wheels). (25) Forward retracting undercarriage frame. (26) Port wing fuel-tanks. (27) Jet pipes. (28) Jet exhaust outlets. (29) Rudder power-controls. (30) Braking parachute—released when landing. (31) Swept-back fin and rudder. (32) Aerials. (33) Elevator power controls. (34) Port elevators. (35) Leading edge of delta wing. (36) Aileron power-controls. (37) Port ailerons. (38) Pitot head for cockpit instruments. (39) Port navigation light.
Span: 99 ft. Length: 97 ft. 1 in. Height: 26 ft. 6 in.

production, and all further work on supersonic bombers to follow the Vulcan and Victor was stopped.

At the time it appeared to be a disastrous policy, even to the most missile-minded enthusiasts. Yet, within two years both America and Russia announced similar plans and it became clear that Britain was still setting the pace in military aviation, as it has done for most of the time since the Royal Flying Corps was formed in 1912.

Where so many people went wrong was in assuming that the R.A.F. intended to abandon piloted warplanes altogether after a few years. In fact, there will simply be a change to different kinds of aeroplane, and some of the possibilities are so exciting that they more than make up for the fact that we are coming to the end of the long line of traditional fighters and long-range bombers.

Before finding out more about these, it would be as well to trace briefly what has happened in military aviation since the end of the 1914–18 War.

For the first six years very little happened, except in America. As we have seen, the British Government was far-sighted enough in 1918 to make the Royal Air Force a completely independent service. This caused a lot of resentment among senior officers of the Army and Navy, who believed that the job of an air force was to put itself at the beck and call of soldiers on the battlefield and fleets at sea. They tried hard to get the Government to change its mind and divide the R.A.F. into Military and Naval components, as in the old days, but without success.

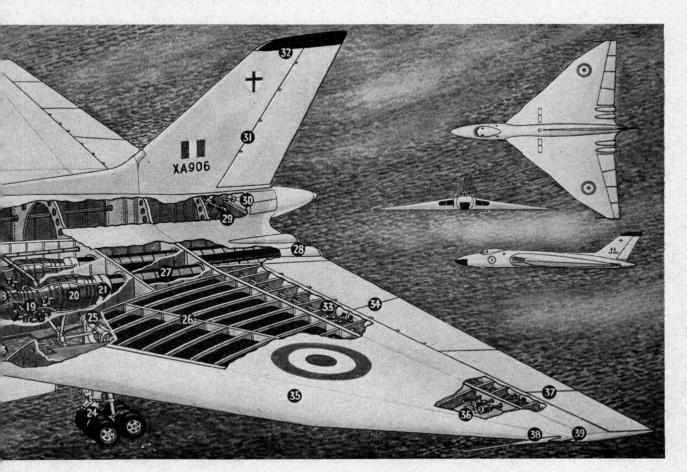

Almost everywhere else in the world—in some cases right up to the present day—air forces remained under army and navy control, which meant that their main duties were defence against enemy attacks, tactical bombing operations in the battlefield (known as "close support") and reconnaissance. Only the R.A.F. was allowed to continue thinking in terms of carrying the war into the homeland of any future enemy by long-range strategic bombing.

One leader of a foreign air force who shared the R.A.F.'s views on the value of strategic bombing was the fiery General "Billy" Mitchell in America. Unfortunately, he was head of the *Army* Air Service and was very junior compared with some of the army and navy officers who saw little value in air power. But he was allowed to buy some Martin MB-2 twin-engined bombers, and promptly used them to sink a number of old German and U.S. battleships at sea, in 1921–23. Claiming this proved that it was sea power and not air power that was useless, he became so out-

spoken that he was court-martialled for insubordination and suspended from duty. Not until the Second World War did America's military chiefs learn that the heavy bomber could be a weapon of the very greatest importance. When they finally realised the truth of Mitchell's claims, they restored him to service with the rank of Major General and awarded him the Congressional Medal of Honour—America's V.C. Unfortunately, he had been dead ten years by then.

Even in Britain it was not easy to persuade the Government and public of the true value of air power. To keep itself in the public eye the R.A.F. put on annual air displays at Hendon aerodrome and these were among the most exciting shows of their kind ever staged. Spectators saw bombers in action, attacking spectacular set pieces on the airfield. Instructors from the Central Flying School showed how aircraft should *not* be flown in "dumb-pupil" crazy-flying acts. Crack fighter squadrons performed aerobatics in

Typical of the highly-advanced supersonic interceptors of to-day is this Saab J 35A Draken of the Royal Swedish Air Force. Airborne within seconds of receiving an alarm, it streaks towards its target at twice the speed of sound, with a pair of deadly Sidewinder air-to-air missiles clutched under its belly. The pilot is guided to-wards the target by radio instructions from ground radar stations. When he gets near to it his own radar, in the Draken's nose, takes over, locking on to the target and telling the pilot automatically when he should fire his missiles.

Martin bombers of the kind used by General "Billy" Mitchell to sink a number of old battleships at sea in 1921–23. This was one of the first demonstrations of the ability of the aeroplane to dominate war at sea.

formation, sometimes with the aircraft tied together; and the latest and best military prototypes were flown over to show what the R.A.F. would like to have if it could afford it.

Until the mid-20's it was given hardly any new equipment. Thousands of aircraft were left over from the war, and these seemed perfectly good enough to the politicians, who thought they had just won the "war to end wars". Actually, there was no time in the 1920's and 30's when the R.A.F. was not fighting somewhere or other. Under a rare piece of imaginative planning in 1922, it had been given complete responsibility for maintaining peace and order in Iraq, where a handful of ancient fighters, bombers and troop transports took the place of thousands of troops. Other squadrons helped in tribal control operations throughout the Middle East.

Ill-informed critics have described this work as inhumane: in fact the opposite was true. If a tribe rebelled or caused trouble, a message was sometimes dropped telling its leaders to behave themselves or their homes would be destroyed. If they still misbehaved, they were given warning that on a certain day the bombing would be carried out, and it was. Sometimes the threat by itself was sufficient.

In any case, there was no need for anybody to be hurt; whereas a punitive expedition on the ground would almost certainly have become involved in heavy fighting.

(Continued on page 142)

Fairey Flycatchers of the Fleet Air Arm attack a dummy ship during the 1924 Hendon Air Display. Their converging runs, from different points of the compass, made one of the most exciting items in a thrill-packed programme.

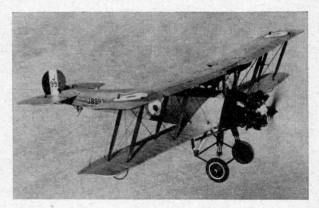

R.A.F. Aircraft between the Wars

What few people realise is that the R.A.F. was never at peace between the two world wars. Always there was a local campaign to fight somewhere, usually in the troubled area of the Middle East. It was not very glamorous work, and the men and machines engaged on it seldom made headlines. But in their day they were as brave and as great as the aircrews and aircraft of the two great wars. Some of the fighters and bombers were relics of the 1914–18 War, like the Sopwith Snipe (*left*) and the D.H. 9A (*top left*). The Avro 504N (*top right*) was a post-war version of the trainer which made the R.A.F. the best-trained air force in the world. Another post-war type was the Vickers Vernon ambulance-transport, a line-up of which, in Iraq, is seen below.

The Fairey Fox (*top left*) was the two-seat day bomber which introduced streamlining into military aviation in the mid-20's. With its neatly-cowled Curtiss engine, it was 50 m.p.h. faster than previous R.A.F. bombers and could outpace any fighter in service, even the aggressive little Gloster Gamecock (*top right*). However, the Gamecock was superbly manœuvrable and was the first aeroplane to survive a 275 m.p.h. dive and 22 turns of a spin.

The Westland Wapiti (*left*) superseded the D.H. 9A as the R.A.F.'s standard general-purpose type in the late 20's and was designed to use as many 9A parts as possible, including the complete wings. Main heavy bomber of the period was the Vickers Virginia, an experimental version of which, shown below, had a gun turret built on the trailing-edge of each upper wing.

The R.A.F. did not enjoy such operations, but they played a major part in keeping trouble to a minimum in places like the North-West Frontier of India, where the tribes had never learned the meaning of the word peace.

The air displays also provided good training, as did the many long-distance flights by flying-boats and formations of smaller aircraft. Typical was the flight from Cairo to the Cape and back by four Fairey IIID biplanes in 1926, one object of which was to survey a possible air route across Africa.

On the technical side, military aircraft design progressed slowly in these years, apart from a switch to metal construction in 1927, some improvement in streamlining and the use of more powerful engines. Designers knew how to build far better aeroplanes than those in service. For example, the Supermarine racing seaplanes with which pilots of the R.A.F. High Speed Flight won the famous Schneider Trophy for Britain in 1931 were beautifully-clean metal monoplanes with a top speed of over 400 m.p.h. Yet the standard single-seat fighters of the time were biplanes capable of only 174 m.p.h.

Then, in 1935, Germany's new leader, Adolf Hitler, revealed the existence of the

The R.A.F. used many of its long-distance training flights to survey possible future air routes. Typical was the flight from Cairo to the Cape and back made in 1926 by four Fairey IIID biplanes.

new *Luftwaffe* (air force) and that his aim was to make it the most powerful in the world. To meet the threat, Britain began a panic expansion of the R.A.F. Great shadow factories were built to speed production of new monoplane fighters and bombers; the motor industry was roped in to help, and the aircraft industry was asked to make superhuman efforts.

They were no ordinary aeroplanes which began to flow from the factories to the R.A.F. and Fleet Air Arm. Fighter Command began to re-equip with the aggressive little Hurricane, with a shattering armament of eight machine-guns, and the 365-m.p.h. Spitfire, based on the 1931 Schneider Trophy

Many great cruises were made also by Supermarine Southampton flying-boats of the kind shown here by the Forth Bridge. In 1927 four of them flew 23,000 miles in formation from Plymouth to Singapore, round Australia, on to Japan and back to Singapore.

Lined up at Calshot are the Supermarine S.6 and S.6B seaplanes which won the Schneider Trophy outright for Britain in 1929 and 1931, and raised the world speed record successively to 357.75 m.p.h. and 407.02 m.p.h.

seaplanes. Bomber Command received the Battle, Blenheim, Wellington and Hampden. Coastal Command could look forward to growing numbers of Sunderland flying-boats. Behind the scenes, designers and technicians were working in secret on still newer and more formidable aircraft, like the mighty four-engined bombers which the Air Ministry had ordered in 1936, at a time when even the *Luftwaffe* thought only in terms of twin-engined aircraft.

When war came, in September 1939, it was clear that aviation would play a major role in it. But few people could have foreseen that the fighting would end in two mushroom clouds of atomic dust over Japan, when just two aeroplanes and two bombs destroyed two cities.

The atomic bomb had given air power complete supremacy over armies and conventional navies; but it was only one of the startling new wartime developments. Jet-propulsion had been perfected and jet-fighters had been used in action in Europe. A whole range of formidable rocket weapons had been developed by Germany and some of them had been fired against Britain. Radar had reached the stage where it could not only give warning of an approaching bomber force, but could enable those same bombers to drop their bombs accurately on targets their crews never saw except as patterns on a cathode-ray tube.

Little wonder that when the war ended in 1945, nobody knew what to expect next or how to plan the most effective and economical peacetime air force. Any hope that there would be no need for air forces in a world of United Nations was dispelled by the Berlin Air Lift of 1948–49 and Korean War of

No place for a forced landing! Hawker Hart day bombers of No. 2 Indian Wing are seen here on patrol among the mountains of Northern India during 1932. At this period there were more Hawker biplanes in the R.A.F. than all other types combined.

Typical of the modern monoplane equipment of the new Luftwaffe, revealed by Hitler in the mid-1930's was the Messerschmitt Bf 109 fighter. Later versions equipped German fighter units throughout World War II.

completely different kind of air power. To complicate matters further, the old wartime German V.1 flying bomb and V.2 rocket had opened up a whole new era of "push-button" weapons which promised to take over the work of traditional fighters and bombers.

It was against this confused background that the British Government made its now-famous decision in 1957 to abandon the development of further aircraft of this kind and devote the efforts of British designers to perfecting weapons of entirely new types. Even now, it is not altogether clear what the R.A.F. of 1970 will be like, but we know enough to paint a most interesting picture of the present and future.

1950–53. The snag was that modern bombers, for example, were becoming so crammed with expensive and highly-advanced equipment that they cost anything up to £2 million each, so air forces could not afford to buy everything they wanted.

If it had been necessary to plan for only an all-out nuclear war it would have been fairly easy; but as such a cataclysmic war became less and less likely the possibility of local or limited wars grew and these demanded a

The key to all present-day international strategy is to prevent a third World War by threatening any would-be aggressor with such an overwhelming counter-attack that he would never dare to start. This is known as a "deterrent policy" and the most important part of any air force is therefore its nuclear attack force of long-range bombers and ballistic missiles. At the moment the finest bombers in service are the R.A.F.'s Vulcan and Victor, which fly so fast and so high that

The aeroplane which, more than any other, marked the start of modern air power was the Boeing Y1B-9 twin-engined monoplane bomber, which had a range of 1,250 miles with a ton of bombs. Here it is being escorted by a Boeing P-26 fighter.

they stand a better chance of eluding the defences than any others in the world. They carry atomic and hydrogen bombs, to which are being added Blue Steel stand-off bombs. These are really guided missiles, shaped like small aeroplanes, which can be launched hundreds of miles from the target and complete the journey on their own. The advantages are that the launching bomber need never approach within range of the target's inner defence ring of fighters and missiles, and that the supersonic stand-off bomb is extremely difficult to intercept.

The Vulcan and Victor are much smaller than the U.S.A.F.'s standard long-range bomber, the B-52 Stratofortress; but this is only because they do not have so far to fly to their potential targets and so need not carry as much fuel. In any case, like most modern fighters and bombers, they can be refuelled in flight by tanker-planes, enabling them to remain airborne for as long as their crews can remain awake and alert.

The latest versions of the Stratofortress are mighty aircraft indeed. The B-52G version, at a take-off weight of 480,000 lb., is the heaviest aeroplane ever flown. In addition to an internal bomb-load it carries a Hound Dog stand-off bomb under each wing, rocket packs to help it fight its way to the target, Quail decoy missiles which are designed to protect it by leading astray fighters and missiles, and several other equally-clever devices. It is being joined in the U.S.A.F.'s Strategic Air Command by supersonic B-58 Hustler medium-bombers, which carry their weapons in the form of under-fuselage pods and can fly at around 1,300 m.p.h. at great heights.

Russia has comparable bombers in the shape of the four-jet subsonic Myasishchev aircraft (N.A.T.O. code name *Bison*) and the new supersonic delta (*Bounder*).

Far more advanced will be the North American B-70 Valkyrie, a six-jet delta-wing bomber designed to cruise at three times the speed of sound (2,000 m.p.h.) for very long

When the first Boeing B-17 Fortress appeared in 1935, it was almost turned down by U.S. Air Corps experts, who preferred to have large numbers of smaller bombers. Yet it went on to become the spearhead of the American bomber offensive in World War II.

distances. At one stage the U.S. Department of Defense decided it did not need any more strategic bombers after the Stratofortress and Hustler, and ordered only a single de-militarised prototype of the Valkyrie. Now, the decision has been changed and the first B-70 should fly in 1963 as a genuine Mach 3 bomber.

At present the bombers are supplemented by Atlas and Titan liquid-propellant inter-continental ballistic missiles (ICBM's). Soon the smaller cheaper solid-propellant Minuteman will be added to these weapons, and there is every reason to believe that Russia has comparable missiles.

The snag with all of these weapons is that they are fired from fixed bases, which could be located and destroyed by an enemy. The fact that most of them will be stored and fired from underground containers reduces their vulnerability; but there are many experts who believe that a force of manned bombers is less vulnerable. Bearing in mind that our own Vulcans and Victors could be airborne within three or four minutes of receiving the warning to go in an emergency, there is a lot of sense in this, and missile-makers are having to think hard to find ways of making their

(Continued on page 148)

Aircraft of World War II

When World War II began in September 1939, the R.A.F. had only 1,911 first-line aircraft, compared with the Luftwaffe's 4,161. Fortunately Britain's aircraft industry proved itself able not only to design the best machines in the world but to produce them in very large numbers. By the time the Battle of Britain opened in August 1940, Fighter Command had 30 squadrons of eight-gun Hawker Hurricanes (*above*) and 19 squadrons of Supermarine Spitfires (*right*). Together they smashed the Luftwaffe from the skies over southern England.

Had we lost the Battle of Britain we should also have lost the war; but the danger was not over. In the Atlantic German submarines threatened to starve Britain into surrender by sinking the convoys bringing food and arms from America and Canada. One of the aircraft which defended the ships was the Short Sunderland flying-boat (*left*). Simultaneously, Bomber Command began to strike back at the enemy homeland, using twin-engined bombers like the Vickers Wellington (*above*).

In due course a new generation of four-motor heavy bombers—the Short Stirling, Handley Page Halifax and Avro Lancaster (*above*)—came along to replace the smaller "twins". With the Fortresses and Liberators of the U.S.A.A.F., they carried on a round-the-clock bomber offensive which brought Germany to its knees.

German fighter pilots fought well against the massed bomber formations of the Allies, in aircraft like the Messerschmitt Bf 109 (*above*) and Focke-Wulf Fw 190; but Hitler ordered that priority be given to fighter-bombers rather than interceptors and eventually they were overwhelmed.

Biggest and heaviest U.S. single-seat fighter was the Republic P-47 Thunderbolt, here seen in action as a fighter-bomber carrying bombs and rockets under its wings. It was used also to escort U.S.A.A.F. bomber formations deep into Germany.

Known as the "Fork-tailed Devil" to the Germans, the twin-engined twin-boom Lightning was used for fighting and photo-reconnaissance. Before the Allied invasion of France in 1944, Lightnings took three million photographs of the enemy coastline.

These two pictures represent the greatest technical developments in air warfare during World War II. The Messerschmitt Me 262 (*above*) was the first jet-fighter used in action. If Hitler had not delayed production for a year, while it was turned into a fighter-bomber, it might have driven the U.S. day-bombers from the air. The Boeing B-29 Superfortress (*right*) was the aircraft used to drop the first atomic bombs on Japan in August 1945.

147

weapons equally mobile and difficult to catch on the ground.

America has Polaris long-range missiles based on submarines at sea and is planning to mount ICBM's on railway trains. But the best idea of all seems to be to lob long-range rockets from aircraft, and that is why the U.S.A.F. has ordered Sky Bolt, a two-stage solid-propellant missile with a devastating nuclear punch, which will be small enough to be carried by the Stratofortress and Hustler—and the R.A.F.'s V-bombers.

When such weapons enter service the defence will be faced with a tremendous task, for they could be fired from any direction, finding their way to the target like the slower stand-off bombs they will replace. Nor do they really need to be launched from high-speed aircraft, for they will be fired far enough from the target for the launching aircraft to have little fear of being shot down. This may well explain why the R.A.F. is not interested in supersonic long-range bombers, for Sky Bolt could be carried and launched equally well by a dual-purpose bomber-transport, which could spend most of its time usefully flying troops and supplies around the world.

Even if strategic bombers disappear within the next ten years, there will be a continuing need for tactical bombers to provide armies with close support in the battlefield, and the R.A.F. will replace its Canberras with squadrons of the new TSR-2 supersonic bomber. We know little about it at the moment, except that it will have two engines of tremendous power, but it is expected to fly at more than 1,500 m.p.h. and to be able to operate from small airstrips in combat areas. So it will be quite an aeroplane!

Already in service with the U.S.A.F. is the single-seat F-105 Thunderchief tactical fighter which can deliver atomic bombs at around 1,300 m.p.h.; but it lacks the short-field capabilities planned for the TSR-2. Nor should we forget the Royal Navy's NA. 39,

for this tremendously-strong strike aircraft can sweep into an attack at around the speed of sound *at sea level*, giving it a great advantage as this puts it "below the reach" of most search radar and anti-aircraft missiles.

If you think that the aircraft carriers on which it is based would not survive long in any future war, remember that they form mobile bases and would have to be found before they could be attacked. By contrast R.A.F. Bomber Command would never expect to make more than one raid from its airfields in Britain, because they would almost certainly have disappeared by the time the bombers returned.

It looks, therefore, as if there is quite a future for piloted bombers, despite the advent of missiles; but what about fighters?

Once again the R.A.F. has equipment second-to-none in the shape of its new Lightning interceptor. With a speed greater than 1,300 m.p.h. and armament of homing missiles and rockets, this twin-engined single-seater could deal with any bomber in service overseas. In its later versions it will be able to operate almost automatically, in all weathers, because the Airpass fire-control radar in its nose-cone makes it virtually a guided missile during an interception.

Details of Airpass's capabilities are secret; but similar types of radar are fitted to U.S. interceptors such as the F-106 Delta Dart, which held the world speed record of 1,525.95 m.p.h. at the time this book was written. With these, the pilot takes off normally and is guided towards the target by radio messages from the ground. When he is within a certain distance of the target he hands over to the fire-control radar in the fighter's nose and simply keeps track of what is happening on his radar screen. The radar picks up the enemy, "locks" on to it and steers the fighter towards it by sending messages to the automatic pilot. Having arrived at the best position for attack, it fires the weapons automatically and then breaks away to avoid the possibility of a

(*Continued on page 157*)

Most efficient bombers in the world today are the R.A.F.'s Victors and Vulcans, which fly so fast and so high that they would stand a better chance of eluding enemy defences than any others. The Handley Page Victor B. Mk. 1, illustrated here, carries underwing fuel tanks for extra range and can be refuelled in flight through the probe extending from above its flight deck.

Like the Victor, the Avro Vulcan can carry atomic or hydrogen bombs and is equipped with all kinds of electronic devices to help it to get past enemy radar, fighters and missiles. It is a huge delta-wing machine, spanning 111 ft. in its Mk. 2 version, which can also carry the Blue Steel stand-off bomb mentioned on page 178.

Typical of the smaller bombers used for tactical support of armies in the field is the Ilyushin Il-28, Russia's counterpart to the R.A.F. Canberra. It is powered by two engines developed from the Rolls-Royce Nene and carries a two-ton bomb-load at up to 580 m.p.h. Many thousands have been built.

Fastest bomber yet to enter service is the Convair B-58 Hustler, which has reached twice the speed of sound (1,320 m.p.h.) during flight tests. The large streamlined pod under its slim fuselage houses its H-bomb warload.

Most formidable single-seat warplane ever built, the Republic F-105 Thunderchief has a Pratt & Whitney J75 turbojet developing 25,000-lb. thrust, a top speed of more than 1,300 m.p.h. and the ability to carry any of the weapons shown here, including atomic bombs. It is intended mainly for close support of ground forces.

These two pictures show the present standard jet-bombers of the Soviet Air Force. Above, with an escort of MiG-17 fighters, is a four-jet Myasishchev bomber known in the West as "Bison". It is believed to span 170 ft., to have a loaded weight of around 350,000 lb. and to be able to carry 4 tons of bombs for 6,000 miles. The twin-engined Tupolev Tu-16 (*left*) is the bomber from which the well-known Tu-104 jet-liner was developed.

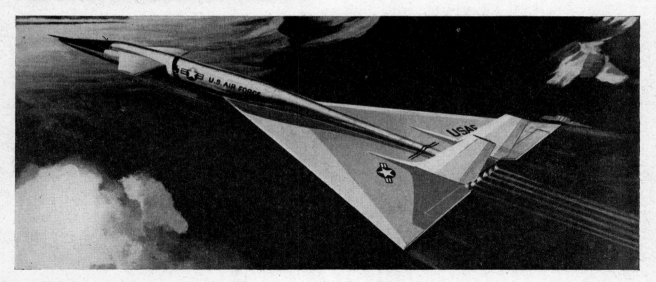

Most advanced bomber yet designed, the North American B-70 Valkyrie is intended to cruise at around 2,000 m.p.h., or three times the speed of sound. Its tail-first delta-wing layout, with six jet-engines mounted at the rear, may well form the basis of a future U.S. supersonic airliner.

THE ENGLISH ELECTRIC LIGHTNING.

Key to the power installation: (1) Air intakes to engines all round centre cone of nose. (2) Air duct to upper and lower engines. (3) Lower Rolls-Royce Avon jet engine with afterburner. (4) Engine starter. (5) Sixteen-stage air compressor. (6) Annular combustion chamber. (7) Three-stage turbine. (8) Upper Rolls-Royce Avon jet engine with afterburner. (9) Upper engine jet-pipe to afterburner. (10) Upper engine afterburner. Here the expanding exhaust gases from the engine are again ignited, giving extra thrust. (11) Lower engine jet pipe to afterburner. (12) Lower engine afterburner. (13) Lower jet exhaust pipe. (14) Upper jet exhaust pipe.

Key to other parts: (15) Connection for drag parachute used for retarding aircraft when landing. (16) Fin and rudder. (17) Swept back tailplane. (18) Tail bumper. (19) Tailplane operating jack. Both tailplanes are moved as elevators. (20) Ventral (under the belly) fuel tank. (21) Port air brake flap (extended). (22) Split flap on trailing edge of swept back wing. (23) Aileron. (24) Main undercarriage wheel retracted. (25) "Hockey-stick"-shaped main wing spar. (26) Cockpit floor over air duct. (27) Nose wheel retracted into space under centre cone. (28) Radar in centre cone. (29) Pitot air pressure booms. (30) De Havilland Firestreak infra-red air-to-air guided missiles being fired.

Span: 34 ft. 10 in. Length: 50 ft. Height: 19 ft. 5 in. Max. speed over 1,300 m.p.h.

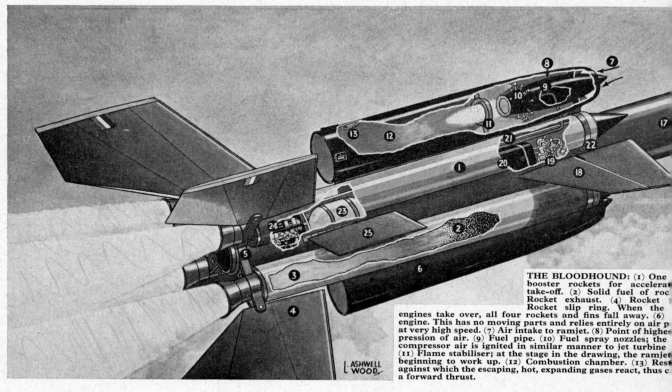

THE BLOODHOUND: (1) One booster rockets for accelera take-off. (2) Solid fuel of roc Rocket exhaust. (4) Rocket Rocket slip ring. When the engines take over, all four rockets and fins fall away. (6) engine. This has no moving parts and relies entirely on air p at very high speed. (7) Air intake to ramjet. (8) Point of highes pression of air. (9) Fuel pipe. (10) Fuel spray nozzles; the compressor air is ignited in similar manner to jet turbine (11) Flame stabiliser; at the stage in the drawing, the ramje beginning to work up. (12) Combustion chamber. (13) Res against which the escaping, hot, expanding gases react, thus c a forward thrust.

L. ASHWELL WOOD.

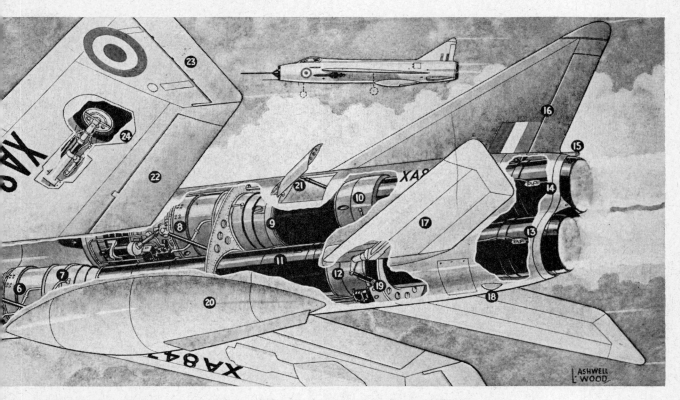

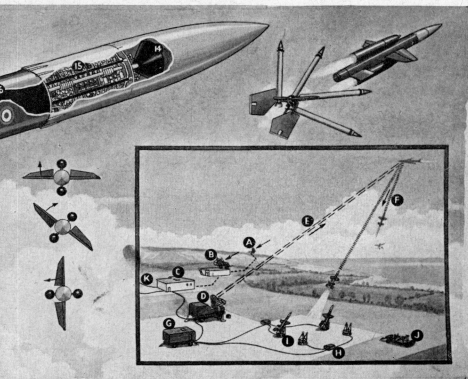

Key to other parts: (14) Radar dish, which picks up the radar reflections from the target. (15) Secret guiding electronics—the brains of the system. (16) Explosive warhead. (17) Outer skin. (18) Moving wing, which performs all the flying directions. (19) Hydraulic wing-operating gear. All the electronic impulses are turned into hydraulic movement by many secret ways. (20) Fuel tank—kerosene. (21) Fuel pipe from weapon to ramjet. (22) Forward slip ring of rocket. (23) Hydraulic (oil) accumulators or reservoirs. (24) Hydraulic (oil) and electrical ground connections before firing. (25) Stabiliser fin.

The Guided Weapon System and the Bloodhound in action: (A) First sign of attack is picked up by Early Warning Radar. (B) When the target is allocated to a particular station, the Tactical Control Radar picks up the plot and follows it. (C) Information is passed electronically to the Tactical Control Centre. (D) The target is allocated to a weapon-firing station and its Target Illuminating Radar. (E) A radar pencil-beam is directed at the target. (F) Reflections from the beam are picked up by the radar dish in the nose of the Bloodhound. (G) The Launch Control Post for firing. (H) Ground power units. (I) Guided weapon launching-ramps. (J) Weapon transport trolley. (K) Connection to other firing stations.

Most modern jet-fighters and bombers can be refuelled in flight to extend their range, and the picture above shows how this is done. It depicts four Cougar fighters of the U.S. Navy topping up their tanks from a Tradewind flying-boat tanker.

From long range we turn to high speed, in the form of the Convair F-106A Delta Dart interceptor (*left*) which set up a world speed record of 1,525.95 m.p.h. just before this book was written. It is a delta-wing machine, developed from the earlier F-102 Delta Dagger and powered by a J75 turbojet.

Beneath it is one of the R.A.F.'s two-seat Gloster Javelin all-weather fighters, carrying a full armament of four de Havilland Firestreak air-to-air homing missiles under its wings.

The sequence of three photographs on this page shows what happens when a Convair F-102A Delta Dagger all-weather interceptor of the U.S.A.F. Air Defense Command launches a salvo of Falcon guided missiles towards an unseen target.

In the first picture, the F-102 is seen beginning its firing run with the missiles concealed behind fast-acting doors in the bottom of its fuselage. When the radar in its nose indicates that the target is coming into range these doors snap open and the missiles are ready to go in less than three seconds.

The pilot sees nothing of the target except as a blip of light on his radar screen. Nor does he fly the aircraft at this stage or fire its weapons, as both jobs are done automatically by the F-102's radar. At a signal from this, the three missiles of the first salvo are fired at 50-millisecond intervals as shown in the centre picture.

In the lower illustration the three Falcons are shown streaking toward their target at more than twice the speed of sound, trailing diamond-shape shock-waves. Two seconds later and the missile-bay doors close, the firing cycle completed. A few more seconds and the missiles have homed on their target, exploding on contact.

Standard interceptor fighters of the Soviet Air Force are MiG-19s of the kind shown here. Unlike the earlier MiG-15 and 17, the 19 is twin-engined, with two small-diameter turbojets mounted side-by-side in its rear fuselage. These give it a speed of around 900 m.p.h. at height. The faster and more powerful MiG-21 is also believed to be in service, but no good photographs of it are available.

Italy's finest contribution to Allied air power is the Fiat G 91 lightweight fighter, powered by a Bristol Siddeley Orpheus turbojet. Many hundreds are being built as fighter-bombers for N.A.T.O. air forces. In addition the German and Italian air forces will use the camera-carrying G 91R reconnaissance version shown above. This retains the normal armament of four 0·5-in. machine-guns in the sides of the fuselage and can dive at supersonic speed.

collision. It only remains for the pilot to fly home for some more weapons.

If radar can do all this—and we know it can also land aircraft completely automatically—why do we need pilots at all? One reason is that fighters sometimes have to go up to take a look at an unidentified aeroplane and only a human pilot might be able to say if it were hostile or friendly. Another reason is that ways might be found of jamming some part of the radar system; but nobody has yet found a method of jamming a human brain.

However, as in the case of bombers, the missiles that the fighters carry are getting faster, more powerful and capable of travelling farther every year. In time there will be little need to launch them from supersonic aircraft and the Americans are already planning to carry and launch their new Eagle nuclear-warhead air-to-air missile from subsonic carrier-planes. The advantage of this is, of course, that such aircraft could stay up much longer than a supersonic fighter and fly out much farther from the target they are defending. In an age of stand-off bombs, launched hundreds of miles from the target, this could make all the difference between success and failure for a defence force.

In fact, there seems no reason why missiles like Eagle should not be carried by the radar picket aircraft which patrol for up to twenty hours at a time and could detect an enemy while it was still far away. In this way we should have a compact "single-package" outer defence ring of very great efficiency, which would operate in conjunction with inner rings of anti-missile missiles.

The fighters and strategic bombers of the future may therefore be very different from anything we have in service today, and the same is true of aircraft used for the vital task of reconnaissance. Most air forces now use camera-carrying versions of their best and fastest fighters and bombers for the job; but this will not be possible if these aircraft are subsonic in the future.

The Hawker Hunter day-fighter is by far the most successful aeroplane ever produced by Britain's aircraft industry. Nearly 2,000 have been built for the R.A.F. and foreign air forces, earning some £200 million from export orders. Although not supersonic in level flight, the Hunter has been perfectly capable of dealing with any bomber in service overseas up to 1960 and it will continue in use as a fighter-bomber for many years, with underwing bombs and rockets supplementing its devastating fixed armament of four 30-mm. cannon. The version illustrated is a Mk. 6 interceptor with four external fuel tanks to increase its endurance.

In America, small radio-controlled aeroplanes, little bigger than models, are in service for reconnaissance duties with the U.S. Army, and a development of this idea, using faster, longer-range pilotless aircraft, seems a possible answer to the problem. We should also remember that when an Earth satellite carrying high-definition T.V. cameras is put into a polar orbit it will pass regularly over every point on Earth, enabling observers on the ground to keep track of what is happening everywhere. The equipment to make this possible may be some years away; but this is another case where a man with a pair of good eyes and some less-intricate instruments might do the job just as well from inside a recoverable satellite of the type now under development.

Side-by-side with these advanced aircraft of tomorrow, air forces will continue to need large and small transports to carry troops, supplies and equipment to wherever they are needed, coastal patrol and anti-submarine bombers, tiny liaison and observation aircraft, machines to tow targets for air-to-air and ground-to-air firing practice, trainers and air-sea rescue aircraft.

However, there is little reason why these should be very different from the highly-advanced types in service or under development today. There may be a gradual swing towards helicopters and other types of VTO aircraft for many tasks, but this will simply be part of the whole pattern of aviation development now that we are awakening to the dangers of aircraft that have to hurtle along 2 miles of concrete before they can claw themselves into the air.

The value of the light helicopter for front-line casualty evacuation duties was first proved during the Korean War when 'copters carried well over 20,000 wounded soldiers to safety, often under fire. The latest type in service for this work is Bell's turbine-powered HU-1A Iroquois, here seen taking on stretchers during an exercise.

Illustrated on this page are three "big boys" of military air transport. Biggest of all is the Douglas C-133 Cargomaster (*top*), a 130-ton giant powered by four 6,000-h.p. turboprops. On 16th December, 1958, it set up an international load-carrying record by lifting 52½ tons to a height of 10,000 ft. When doing so, it required a take-off run of only 4,500 ft.

Next in size in the U.S.A.F.'s transport force is the Lockheed Hercules, the ski-equipped C-130D version of which is seen (*centre*) at the South Pole. Largest machine ever to touch down at the bottom of the world, it has four 3,750-h.p. turboprop engines and can haul more than 25 tons of payload, including large vehicles and guided missiles.

Most modern military transports can be used to drop heavy equipment by parachute in places where landings cannot be made, and this technique is being demonstrated by the Blackburn Beverley (*bottom*). Although it looks cumbersome, this piston-engined freighter can airlift loads of up to 20 tons and operate into forward airstrips no more than 1,000 ft. long.

Few flying-boats remain in first-line duty with major air forces, but the U.S.A.F. uses large numbers of Grumman Albatross amphibians for air-sea rescue work. Some have sprung skids under their hull and wing floats, enabling them to land on ice or snow in polar regions.

One of the least-publicised, but vital roles performed by the American-built version of the Canberra is that of target-towing. Here a B-57E is seen streaming a banner target which will be let out many hundreds of feet for air-to-air firing practice by fighters.

No better illustration of modern sea power could be found than this view of the U.S.S. *Forrestal*, one of America's huge 76,000-ton attack carriers, with part of her brood parked on deck. They include Skywarrior atom-bombers, Demon interceptors and general-purpose piston-engined Skyraiders.

The three main tasks of a modern carrier force are to attack enemy targets ashore and afloat, put ashore troops and supplies by helicopter and protect the fleet from enemy attack. The principal strike aircraft of the Royal Navy at the present time is the Supermarine Scimitar, one of which is seen here firing a salvo of rockets from under-wing launchers. A single-seater, powered by two Avon turbojets, the Scimitar can fly almost at the speed of sound at sea level and is able to carry nuclear weapons.

Air Power Afloat

On this and the next few pages are illustrated the weapons of present-day naval aviation.

Largest aircraft yet built for carrier operations is the North American A3J Vigilante. It is a two-seater, spanning 50 ft. and powered by two 15,000-lb. thrust General Electric J79 turbojets. These give it a top speed of more than 1,300 m.p.h. at height. An interesting feature of the Vigilante is that its bombs are ejected out of the tail from a linear bomb-bay, consisting of a tunnel inside the rear fuselage.

Britain's counterpart to the Vigilante is the Blackburn NA. 39, a much smaller two-seat strike aircraft powered by two 10,000-lb. thrust de Havilland Gyron Junior turbojets. Although not intended to fly at supersonic speed, the NA. 39 is one of the few aircraft strong enough for sustained flight just below the speed of sound at sea level and would thus be able to make highly-effective "under-the-radar" attacks with nuclear weapons. It is shown here on the deck lift of H.M.S. *Victorious*, with wings and nose folded and air-brakes wide open at the tail.

The helicopter's assault role is depicted by these members of a Royal Marine Commando boarding a Whirlwind helicopter on the flight deck of an aircraft carrier. First ship specially adapted for this type of work is H.M.S. *Bulwark*, which carries a complete Commando, with all necessary helicopters, equipment and supplies, ready for putting ashore at any trouble spot at a moment's notice. The technique was first used at Suez in 1956, with considerable success. Having delivered their troops, the Whirlwinds were able to fly casualties speedily back to the carrier for medical attention.

The U.S. Marines also have experimented on a large scale with the use of helicopters for beach-head assault. Here a Sikorsky HUS-1 (S-58) takes off as a flying crane with a load of supplies, while deck crews prepare a twin-engined HR2S-1 (S-56) to ferry 20 fully-equipped troops ashore. As big as a DC-3, the HR2S-1 combines the load-carrying capacity of this veteran airliner with the versatility of a helicopter. Stripped of its bulky fuselage, it becomes the S-60 Skycrane, illustrated on page 86.

One of the main snags with radar is that it is a "line-of-sight" system. Radar waves do not bounce back from the upper atmosphere as do radio waves, and the only way of seeing "over the horizon" is to build taller aerials. The tallest ones of all are the airborne radar scanners carried by early-warning aircraft like this Gannet A.E.W. Mk. 3. Circling high above the fleet, it is able to detect approaching enemy aircraft or ships while they are still many miles away and direct fighter and strike aircraft to intercept the attackers.

On this page are shown some of the interceptors built to provide atomic-age protection for ships of the British and U.S. Navies. On the right is a de Havilland Sea Vixen, manned by a crew of two and powered by two Rolls-Royce Avon turbojets which enable it to dive at supersonic speed. In addition to the four Firestreak air-to-air missiles carried under its wings, it has two retractable trays under its nose, each containing 14 air-to-air rockets.

With the Sea Vixen to provide all-weather and night fighter cover, and the Scimitar (*left*) for daylight interception duties, the Royal Navy is extremely well equipped. A far more powerful fighter in production for the U.S. Navy is the McDonnell F4H-1 Phantom II (*above*)—a two-seater with two J79 turbojets and an armament of four Sparrow missiles, carried semi-submerged under its fuselage and wings.

Until the Phantom is ready for operation, the main U.S. Navy interceptor is the Chance Vought Crusader (*left*). A single-seater, powered by a Pratt & Whitney J57 turbojet, the Crusader has a top speed of around 1,200 m.p.h. in its latest F8U-2N form and is armed with four Sidewinder missiles, mounted on pylons on each side of its forward fuselage. It has a variable-incidence wing (see page 121).

Although comparatively small by U.S. standards, with a displacement of only 30,000 tons, H.M.S. *Victorious* is second-to-none in terms of fighting efficiency. The twenty-year-old carrier was completely reconstructed during the 1950's and was the first British carrier to enter service with a fully-angled deck, as well as two steam catapults and mirror landing aids. Her high-powered radar, the drum-shape aerial of which can be seen above the bridge, is able to detect aircraft at considerable range and show their position simultaneously in range, bearing and height.

This official artist's impression depicts a possible aircraft carrier of the future. It consists of a giant submarine, the flight deck being underneath the top plating, so that aircraft are launched through ports, rather like torpedoes. Whether we shall ever see such a vessel, or whether carriers and aircraft will give way to missile-armed submarines, only the future will tell.

Aircraft carriers may be big in terms of shipping, but they are terribly small compared with a land aerodrome. This fact is well brought out by photographs like that on the right, which shows the tiny size of the landing area on even the U.S.S. *Independence*, one of the largest carriers in the world. Fortunately, since the invention of the angled deck, pilots who miss the arrester wires with their deck-hook can fly on over the side and go round for a second attempt. The standard of precision normally achieved is shown by the mass of tyre marks between the arrester wires on the white-painted portion of the landing deck. Also visible in this picture is the mirror landing aid, off the port side of the deck, which has replaced the war-time deck landing officer or "batsman".

Rockets for Research

WHEN you hear the word "rocket" you probably think of a military missile or of one of the monsters used for launching satellites. But there are, of course, many other kinds, ranging from the type that give us noisy pleasure on Guy Fawkes Day, to those attached to lifelines at Coastguard stations.

Rockets are also used extensively in aircraft research. Their ability to develop great power reliably and relatively cheaply ensures their use wherever high speeds are required. For example, when North American Aviation test pilot George Smith baled out of his crippled aircraft while it was travelling at between 700 and 800 m.p.h. and survived, his exploit was studied with interest by those people whose job it is to develop means of escaping from crashing aircraft. For Smith was one of the first, if not the very first, pilot to bale out of an aircraft travelling faster than sound and live to describe the experience.

To learn more about this escape, a steel-and-rubber dummy of the test pilot was made for use in experiments duplicating the super-

A steel-and-rubber dummy is lowered into a rocket-powered sled for supersonic ejection tests. The "arrow" protruding from this dummy's chest is the aerial for a tiny transmitter inside him.

The badly damaged dummy is examined after one test.

sonic ejection. Even if the use of a full-size aeroplane had been possible, close observation of the sequence of events would have been extremely difficult. So, a full-size section of the nose of the aircraft, including the cockpit, was made and mounted on a sled. To propel the sled special rockets were fitted and whoosh—down it went at 700 m.p.h. along a specially constructed track. The tests seemed to indicate that Smith's survival had been due largely to luck, and so urgent attention was given to the task of developing a reliable emergency system for the new U.S. Air Force supersonic "Century Series" of jet interceptors and bombers. For their F-106, Convair built an improved sled representing the front of the fuselage of this 1,000-m.p.h.-plus interceptor. Experiments with this culminated in the development of a rocket-powered "aerial bobsled" seat.

This is how this novel seat works. For normal flight the pilot sits upright, but in an emergency the seat rotates backwards 80 degrees and is then shot out of the aircraft by a rocket. An automatic sequencing system, actuated by an altimeter, then releases a small drag parachute to slow the seat down before

A rocket-powered model ready for a test flight concerning wing-tip mounted pods.

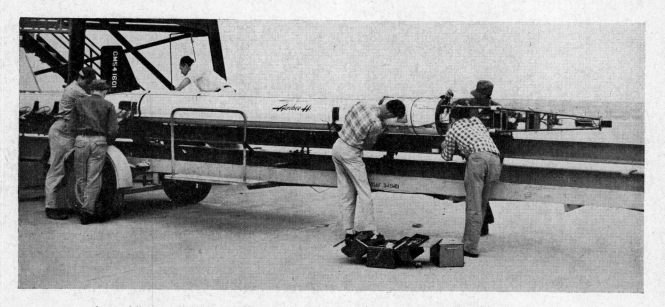

Assembling an Aerobee-Hi research rocket at Holloman Air Force Base launching site.

the main 'chute is deployed. On the way down the pilot's seat belt releases, allowing the seat to fall away.

Similar seats, working on a somewhat simpler principle have been developed in Britain for use in our supersonic aircraft.

Rockets are also used extensively to propel small models of projected aircraft at great speeds to enable their behaviour to be studied in free flight.

Another important use for rockets is for high altitude and meteorological research. Many countries, including Russia, fired "met" rockets in the nineteen-twenties and early thirties, but twenty years were to pass before they were used on an effective scale. In August 1944, the Americans launched a Wac Corporal to a height of 44 miles to start the most ambitious programme of research at high altitudes ever undertaken. In 1946 about 100 captured German V.2's were allotted to this research work.

Some improved rockets were obviously required and from the Wac Corporal there developed the Aerojet Aerobee, which can carry payloads of 150 lb. up to around 100 miles. This is a relatively simple rocket, guided initially by rails until its speed is sufficient for its fins to be effective, and has turned out to be one of the most useful

After ejection, a small parachute slows the seat so that the main 'chute can be deployed. The seat drops away automatically.

rockets ever produced. It was with Aerobees that some of the first tentative experiments into the effects of weightlessness and other aspects of space flight were made.

In an early experiment two monkeys, named Pat and Mike, were carried up to 37 miles at 2,000 m.p.h., ejected automatically when the Aerobee started its fall back to earth, and then landed safely by parachute.

In later, more ambitious experiments, monkeys were successfully fired to greater heights. In these the monkeys were anaesthetised before take-off and strapped down by nylon netting on sponge rubber couches. They were each provided with a tiny face mask for a supply of oxygen, and attached to their bodies were various instruments which enabled records to be made of their blood-pressure, heart beats and breathing.

In other experiments mice were fired aloft. These were conscious, and an automatic cine camera obtained some of the first pictures of the reactions of weightlessness. During the three-minute period of this condition the mice floated about, unable to distinguish "up" from "down" and apparently as much at ease when upside down as when up the other way.

Landing safely. A survival kit and life raft attached to the harness swing below the pilot as he descends. During a descent from high altitude the life raft will inflate automatically, ready for immediate use if the pilot lands in water.

169

From the V.2 there developed the bigger and more elaborate Viking research rocket, possibly the finest research vehicle of its type ever produced. It was powered by a motor of 20,500-lb. thrust, and took off vertically from a simple platform. To keep the rocket steady during the initial stages of the flight, before the air speed was great enough for the fins to become effective, the motor was mounted on a gimbal. Acting under the control of gyroscopes the motor moved, thus deflecting the whole exhaust stream. This method of control has proved very reliable and is now used almost universally on large rockets. It is also the reason why big rockets do not require the large fins so prominently predicted in science fiction stories a few years ago. The Viking could carry a maximum of 2,000 lb. of instruments and with smaller payloads could reach heights of over 100 miles. In addition to increasing our knowledge of the composition and conditions in the upper reaches of the atmosphere, a series of spectacular high altitude photographs from cameras mounted in the tail fins were obtained, showing the appearance of the Earth from heights of over 100 miles.

In Britain the Skylark rocket has been developed for high altitude research. This is a relatively small rocket, designed to carry a payload of 100 to 150 lb. to altitudes of about 100 miles, and it has proved very reliable. Experiments have included the ejection of "window", strips of metallic foil, to permit the measurement of high altitude wind speeds, and the exploding of grenades to provide information on air temperature and density.

While rockets of this type are making their brief one-and-only flight to the fringe of space, the information gained is transmitted to the ground by a method called telemetering. It works this way: As many as fifty reporting devices are connected to a single radio transmitter, which broadcasts the reading obtained from each in quick succession as a series of jumbled sounds. A receiver on Earth picks up the tangle of signals, sorts them out, and prints the information as a series of spidery wavelike lines on a roll of paper. Each line represents the finding of a particular instrument, giving air pressure, temperature, radiation intensity and so on.

The useful life of the rockets, which are not cheap, is only a matter of minutes and to be really comprehensive information is often required over much longer periods of time. This is where artificial satellites come into

A Skylark soars spacewards. This British rocket has proved exceptionally reliable and the Americans have decided to purchase some for special experiments.

U.S. Navy Viking research rocket. This rocket was developed into the bottom booster for the Vanguard series of satellites.

their own, for once launched these continue to orbit effortlessly for weeks, months, or even years.

But for some experiments, such as simultaneous "spot" checks on the temperature and pressure at certain altitudes over different parts of the earth, the simple research rocket still has its uses.

*

Military Missiles

Air-to-Air

MODERN bombers fly so fast that an attacking fighter would probably have time to aim at them only once. Even then the period would be very short, hardly long enough for machine-gun bullets or cannon shells to be effective. And yet, with bombers capable of carrying hydrogen-bombs equal to many millions of tons of ordinary

Two de Havilland Firestreak "heat-seeking" air-to-air missiles are carried by the English Electric Lightning interceptor.

high explosive, every one *must* be destroyed before it reaches its target. To help fighters to do this, air-to-air missiles have been developed. As the name implies, these are rockets designed to be carried by aircraft and fired at airborne targets.

First missile in this category to be bought by the Royal Air Force was the Fairey Fireflash. This is unusual in that the missile itself is really an unpowered dart. It is accelerated rapidly by means of two powerful boosters which detach when exhausted, leaving the missile proper coasting towards its target.

The Fireflash, used for training purposes, is a beam rider—that is, it flies along a pencil radar beam transmitted from the launching aircraft. This beam follows the aircraft being attacked like an invisible searchlight beam; the missile flying within the beam is inevitably guided towards its target. When it approaches within a lethal distance of the quarry a proximity fuse explodes the warhead.

Later missiles are not only powered, usually by a solid-propellant charge, but have improved methods of guidance. Three such missiles are the de Havilland Propellers Firestreak, the standard Royal Air Force weapon, and the U.S. Sidewinder and GAR-2A Falcon, which are designed to home on the infra-red or heat rays emitted by the engines of an aircraft. This guidance system is particularly effective as the source becomes stronger the nearer the missile gets, thus increasing its accuracy. The Sidewinder has the distinction of being the first such missile to see active service and in actual operations off Formosa 14 Chinese

Batteries of Nike-Ajax surface-to-air anti-aircraft missiles, such as this one, stand guard in Alaska, Greenland, Germany and around 40 cities and targets in the United States.

To be effective, an anti-aircraft missile must be capable of instant readiness whatever the weather. Here an English Electric Thunderbird undergoes a low temperature test.

Virtually a pilotless interceptor, the Boeing Bomarc surface-to-air missile has a range of 250 miles.

Mig-17s were reported destroyed in a single day by Sidewinders fired from Sabres of the Chinese Nationalist Air Force.

Most potent of all air-to-air missiles is the Douglas Genie which, although it is not guided, carries an atomic warhead.

Surface-to-Air

Missiles in this category are nearly all anti-aircraft weapons and back up, or in some cases supplant, the air-launched missiles.

Typical of such anti-aircraft missiles are the U.S. Nike-Ajax, Nike-Hercules and Raytheon Hawk, the Swiss Contraves Oerlikon Type 56, and the French Sud SE 4400.

Intended to do the work of artillery and close support aircraft over ranges up to 20 miles, the Martin Lacrosse is a simple, highly accurate, surface-to-surface weapon which can be controlled from a front-line position remote from its launching point.

Boosted by some 300,000-lb. thrust from its first-stage motors, a 6,000-mile range Martin Titan Intercontinental Ballistic Missile takes off on a test firing.

The standard British home defence missile is the Bristol Bloodhound, operated by the Royal Air Force. Powered by two ramjets, the Bloodhound has a greater range than the conventional rocket propelled weapons, in this case "several score" miles. It employs semi-active homing—that is, the missile picks up and homes on to reflected radiation from the target, the latter being "illuminated" by powerful signals from a ground radar.

A standard Bloodhound Firing Unit consists of two groups of eight missiles served by its own Sting-Ray radar. This arrangement permits from one to eight Bloodhounds to be fired simultaneously at a particular aircraft, while the other eight could be homed on to a different target.

Longer in range than the Bloodhound is the Boeing Bomarc. Looking very much like a pilotless interceptor—which is exactly what it is—a single Bomarc can guard more than 100,000 square miles of territory. Integrated into the United States Air defence system, and capable of being launched by remote command from underground control centres 1,500 miles distant from the missile site, the Bomarc has an extremely efficient terminal-homing target-seeking device, permitting it even to home from 70,000 ft. on to a target flying at 50 ft.

Surface-to-Surface

These are the "heavy bombers" of the missile squadrons, and are the direct descendants of the German V.2 missile of the 1939–45 War. Included are short or medium range tactical missiles such as the U.S. Army Honest Johns, Sergeants, Pershings and Redstones and the still secret British Blue Water.

In the intermediate range fall the Thor, the Russian missiles illustrated opposite and Jupiter.

Overshadowing these are the mighty ICBM's—Inter-Continental Ballistic Missiles —which, with their ranges of more than

A Martin Mace tactical guided missile caravan rolls across country on a training mission. The Mace has a range of over 650 miles and can be used for either high-altitude missions or low-level attacks when these offer a better chance of success.

6,000 miles and ability to carry deadly megaton hydrogen-bomb warheads, were at one time thought to be the ultimate or most deadly weapons that could ever be developed.

First ICBM to see service in the West was the giant Convair Atlas. When originally planned, the Atlas weighed over 200 tons, but developments leading to a lightweight warhead enabled this to be reduced by half to a mere 100 tons or so. The Atlas is unusual in that it has a centrally-mounted sustainer motor developing 60,000-lb. thrust, flanked each side by a booster. All three motors fire at take-off, the boosters dropping away after

three minutes. A novel feature of the missile is its skin which is so thin that it has to be "blown-up" like a balloon to prevent it collapsing as the propellants are consumed.

Disadvantages of the Atlas are that, being launched from above ground, it is a vulnerable target and, using liquid propellants, it is not practicable to keep it in a state of instant preparedness. Both these drawbacks will be overcome by the Minuteman missile now under development in the United States. These will be smaller, lighter, simpler, cheaper, quicker. Some will be sunk in deep wells; unmanned, silent sentinels

This picture, taken in Moscow in 1957, is one of the few available of Russian military missiles. The weapons depicted are 75 ft. long and are thought to have a range of about 450 miles. They may have been joined since by more advanced missiles.

Two Hound Dog "stand-off" bombs can be seen under the wing of this Boeing B-52 bomber. These are, in effect, powered bombs, designed to be released while the carrier bomber is still many hundreds of miles from the target, and therefore, beyond reach of many of the defences.

ready to be launched at a moment's notice. Others, it is planned, will be mounted on railway trucks, road transporters or barges; this mobility being designed to prevent a potential enemy from knowing where they are and so being able to destroy them.

Special Missiles

In addition to the three classes of missiles described so far, there is an ever increasing variety of specialised missiles. These range from small rockets capable of being carried and fired by one man, to "stand-off" bombs such as the Avro Blue Steel and North American Hound Dog, released from carrier bombers many hundreds of miles from their targets. Other missiles such as the U.S.A.F. Quail, designed to be released from bombers being attacked by rockets, carry electronic countermeasures equipment which reflects radar waves in exactly the same way as the

bomber, so that the rockets home on the decoy instead of the bomber. Special anti-submarine missiles have been developed which after entering the water act like self-homing torpedoes. The U.S. Navy Polaris, capable of delivering a hydrogen-bomb warhead of tremendous destructive power over a range of 1,200 miles, is designed to be fired from submarines while they are submerged!

Most difficult missiles of all to design—and not yet perfected—are those such as the U.S. Nike Zeus. These fantastic missiles are intended for use against ICBM's. Carrying nuclear warheads they will rise at terrific speed to intercept an approaching rocket while it is still hundreds of miles up in space, where its destruction will do no harm. Zeus itself should also be able to intercept a hostile satellite if necessary. When this becomes possible the day of Dan Dare warfare will have arrived; fact will have overtaken fiction.

Satellites in the Sky

THE year 1957 witnessed an event as important as the invention of steam power, electricity and the taming of the atom. The world's first artificial satellite was launched. The space age began.

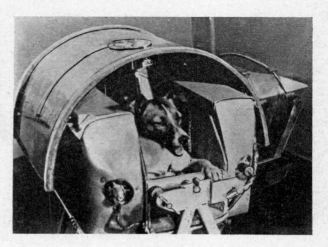

Above. Sputnik I, the world's first artificial satellite, launched by Russia on 4th October, 1957. *Above right.* Schoolchildren in Moscow listening to the "bleeps" from Sputnik I. These were the first man-made sounds to be transmitted from space. *Right.* Laika, a Russian dog which orbited the Earth in a satellite for a week in 1957. This was the first experiment with life in orbit.

The successful launching of America's first satellite, the Explorer I, on 31st January, 1958.

Scientists had long realised that the rocket would one day take them into space. Serious suggestions were made at the turn of the century first by a German inventor, Hermann Ganswindt, followed soon afterwards by a Russian scientist, Konstantin E. Ziolkowsky, who in 1903 published a paper indicating that a rocket could operate in a vacuum.

In 1907 Robert Esnault-Pelterie, the French pioneer, commenced a mathematical investigation into the possibilities of space flight.

The 1939–45 War saw the development of the V.2 long-range rocket, and it was evident that the dream of space flight would before long become fact.

When the International Geophysical Year was arranged for 1958, America announced her proposal to launch a series of small satellites as part of her contribution to the co-ordinated study of the Earth by the scientists of fifty nations. To launch their satellite, called Vanguard, the Americans designed a modest rocket 72 ft. long and weighing a little over 10 tons. To give the required orbital speed of around 17,000 m.p.h., the rocket had three steps, or stages, and the motor in the lower, main-booster stage, developed 27,000-lb.thrust.

This was only about half the power of the V.2 rocket used by the Germans during the 1939–45 War, so it was evident that the Vanguard was a relatively small vehicle, intended to orbit the smallest practicable satellite. During its development, full details of both successes and failures were given, whereas a brief announcement by the Russian Professor Leonid Sedov in 1955 that his country too intended launching satellites was soon forgotten.

Thus, in 1957, although technicians were half expecting a satellite, there was world-wide surprise when, on 4th October, the first one was launched not in the West from America, but in the East from Russia. Almost as much of a surprise as that caused by the satellite itself was its weight of 184 lb. This

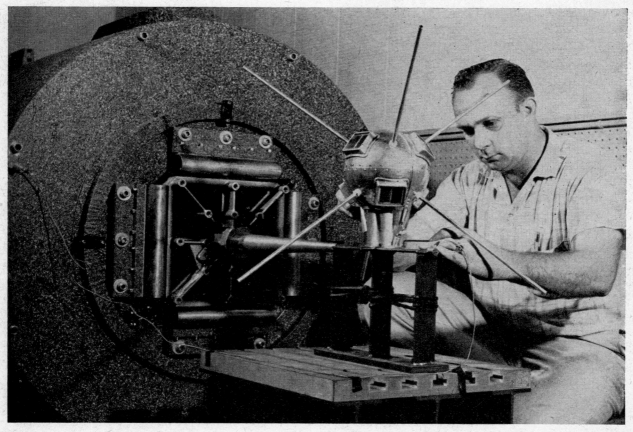

Vanguard I. This tiny test satellite, 6½ in. in diameter and weighing only 3¼ lb. was launched into orbit in March, 1958. Since then the six solar cells in the outer skin have converted sunlight into electricity to provide sufficient power to keep its tiny transmitter working continuously.

was nearly ten times heavier than the planned weight of the American Vanguard, and very much heavier than anybody had predicted for the first man-made artificial moon. The satellite orbited the Earth at a height varying from 142 miles to 588 miles, the time taken for one revolution being ninety-six minutes. As it travelled around in the vacuum of space, a tiny radio transmitter telemetered back details of the pressure, temperature and other data. Making a noise sounding like a series of beep, beep, beeps, this sound from space was undoubtedly one of the most exciting ever heard.

The Sputnik, as the Russians called their satellite, was the first real step to space exploration and interplanetary flight. A man-made object was travelling in space, at a speed and height greater than anything previously launched by man.

The fact that the satellite continued to circle the Earth, hour after hour, day after day, without any power, puzzled many people, but the principle which kept it there is very simple. If a body outside the atmosphere is given a sufficiently high speed parallel with the surface of the Earth, it will remain in space, just balanced between its centrifugal force—trying to make it fly away—and the Earth's gravitational pull—trying to tug it down. A body cannot do this close to the surface of the Earth, because the friction of the air would either slow it down or melt it.

A month later the Russians launched a second, bigger satellite, Sputnik II. Once again the heavy weight of the satellite—about half a ton—amazed technicians. But this was not all, for the satellite carried a live dog, Laika, of the husky-type breed. Delicate instruments measured the dog's breathing, its heart beats and temperature and then transmitted the results to listening stations on the Earth. It was a momentous event—as important as the first fiery ascent of a Montgolfier hot-air balloon, or the first flight of the historic Wright Flyer, described earlier in this book—the world was witnessing the first prolonged flight through space by a living creature.

Contained in a pressurised, air-conditioned compartment and supplied automatically with food and water, the dog orbited the Earth for a week before dying when the air supply gave out. It was sad that technical development did not enable this dog to be returned safely,

but comfort can be gained from the fact that death should have come quickly and painlessly.

The Russian successes came as a profound shock in the United States, and behind the scenes rocket technicians laboured feverishly to make up lost time in a race which many felt that America could have won if the starting signal had been given a little earlier.

The first attempt, made in December with a Vanguard, was a spectacular failure as the rocket exploded a few seconds after lifting off. Because of the tremendous pre-launching publicity given with typical American brashness, the failure received equally tremendous publicity in newspaper headlines throughout the world.

Up to this time the United States authorities had endeavoured to keep their I.G.Y. satellite activities quite divorced from their military programme, but in their anxiety to get something into orbit, they turned to Dr. Wernher von Braun, the German V.2 designer, now

Nicknamed the "Paddle Wheel" satellite, the U.S. Explorer VI, was launched on 7th August, 1959. The paddles are covered with solar cells that turn sunlight into electricity to provide power for the radio transmitters and other instruments.

resident in the United States and at that time working for the U.S. Army Ballistic Missile Agency at Huntsville, Alabama.

The result was that within three months from being given the official go-ahead, Explorer I was in orbit as America's first satellite. Small by comparison with the Russian Sputniks, the Explorer was a slim pencil-shape, 80 in. long by 6 in. diameter, weighing 30 lb. It was launched by a special 65,000-lb. four-stage version of the Army's test rocket Jupiter C.

A month later the Vanguard team managed to launch a tiny 3¼-lb., 6½-in.-diameter satellite into an orbit ranging from 409 to 2,453 miles. Although small, this satellite is of interest because of its solar batteries inset in the polished aluminium sphere. Converting sunlight into electrical energy these were still supplying power to the radio in the middle of 1960, after over two years in space. A few days later, after an intervening failure, America launched her third satellite, Explorer III, similar to Explorer I.

On 15th May, 1958, the Russians launched their third satellite, Sputnik III, a real space laboratory weighing 1½ tons, crammed full of a wide variety of instruments.

Other satellites were then launched with such rapidity that it became difficult to keep track of them all. Notable was the orbiting, just before Christmas 1958, of an entire Atlas ICBM. Some 80 ft. long and 10 ft. in diameter this satellite had the bulk of two railway coaches placed end to end. Instrumentation included two tape recorders and playback transmitters. These received and recorded messages from the ground, and then rebroadcast the messages on receipt of a second signal from the ground. The first voice to be heard from space was that of President Eisenhower, who broadcast a message of goodwill to the peoples of the world.

With satellites barely beyond the "Wright Flyer" stage of development, scientific curiosity began reaching out for the Moon.

On 14th September, 1959, the Russian Lunik II scored a direct hit on the Moon. Upon impact it scattered metal pennants and discs over the surface, replicas of which are shown above assembled into frangible spheres.

Lunik III, the Russian satellite which obtained the first pictures of the rear face of the Moon, which is always turned away from the Earth.

The first Moon probe was launched by the Americans from Cape Canaveral. Called Pioneer I, the launching vehicle just failed to develop the required power, with the result that after stretching 70,000 miles into deep space, far higher than anything previously launched by Man, the glass-fibre encased satellite halted and then fell back towards the Earth, where atmospheric friction gave it a fiery end. In January 1959, the Russians launched their Lunik I, which coasted past the Moon and into orbit round the Sun. The first artificial planet, it is sometimes referred to as Mechta, or Planet Ten, as there are nine natural planets, of which Earth is one. Lunik II, launched a few months afterwards, scored a direct hit on the Moon, a feat ensured of a notable niche in history, for with it Man made physical contact with another world for the first time.

The same year Lunik III went round the Moon, taking photographs of the rear face which is permanently turned away from us. The photographs were automatically processed and developed inside the satellite and then transmitted by television apparatus back to recording stations in the Soviet Union. When reprocessed back into pictures, we were able to see, for the first time, what the hidden face looks like.

Already these satellites, small and crude by comparison with the bigger and better ones now under development, are revealing hitherto hidden secrets of the space around the Earth. One of the most important discoveries was the existence of two belts of radiation surrounding the Earth, forced into the shape of a doughnut by the Earth's magnetic field. Now called the Van Allen belts, their intensity is such that if they extended deep into space they would present a serious, if not insurmountable, handicap to manned interplanetary flight.

Other satellites have provided new information on the exact shape of the Earth, cosmic radiation, solar radiation and micro-meteoric intensity.

The first tentative experiments have been made towards the development of weather survey satellites. The U.S. Vanguard II crudely measured the variation in cloud coverage by means of optical telescopes focussed on specially-developed light detectors. Such information will in future be of great value to meteorologists and permit forecasts of an accuracy not attainable today.

Man in Space

EVER since Goddard fired the world's first liquid propellant rocket in 1926, the ultimate aim of rocket scientists has been to put a man into space.

It is difficult to imagine what it is like in space because the conditions there are so utterly different from those to which we become automatically accustomed on the surface of the Earth. The atmosphere which provides us with the oxygen for us to breathe acts also as a gigantic protective mantle. It protects the surface from all but a few dozen of the 75,000 *million million* meteors with which the Earth is bombarded each day. It provides a pressure without which our blood would boil. It protects us from the searing radiation emanating from the Sun and outer space which would otherwise boil away the sea and roast us alive. In orbit, Man will also be weightless, a condition so alien to everyday

Russian airman Milhailov undergoing training for future flights through space. He is in a chamber in which the pressure is about to be reduced to the almost complete vacuum experienced in space. In contrast with the high technical standard of most of his equipment, his legs appear to be covered with sheepskin trousers!

The arm of the huge man-carrying centrifuge of the Aviation Acceleration Laboratory at Johnsville, in America.

life that it is almost impossible to reproduce it experimentally, even for short periods, to give us some idea of what it will be like.

It is thus apparent that for a man to venture into space he will have to be provided with a cabin containing the necessities of life, oxygen, pressure, protection from radiation, in much the same way that a goldfish has to be

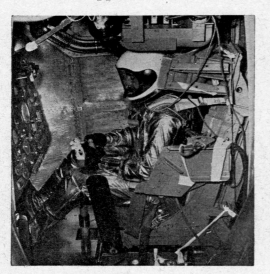

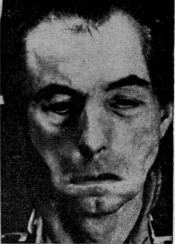

(*Left*) Test pilot Scott Crossfield prepares himself for a simulated flight into space in the centrifuge gondola. At the start of a space-flight, astronauts will be subjected to accelerations of several "g" making them feel heavier than normal.

The right-hand picture shows the face of a volunteer being subjected to 10 g.—ten times his usual weight—and may be compared with his normal face (*centre*).

186

This television picture was obtained during a simulated five-day journey to the Moon. The volunteer frequently donned dark glasses to shade his eyes from the bright glare of the simulator lighting.

provided with a bowl of its natural environment before it can survive in the alien conditions of a family living-room.

Research into various aspects of high-speed and high-altitude flight provided a firm basis from which to extend into space. For example, when intercepting an enemy aircraft a fighter pilot may have to manœuvre so violently that several "g"s will be imposed. This tends to drain blood from his head, causing temporary blindness and ultimately loss of consciousness. Very often, the pilot who can withstand the highest "g"s—the one who can make the tighter turn—will be the victor.

It is thus important to find out how many "g"s pilots can withstand without harm, and to see if equipment can be designed to assist them to tolerate even higher loads. For this purpose immense machines called man-carrying centrifuges have been built in Britain, America and Russia. These machines consist of long arms, supporting a gondola at the free end, which can be rotated at high speed to impart "g" loads and thus reproduce the conditions in a manœuvring aircraft.

Iceberg temperatures, made by a mountain of ice, fail to chill the wearer of a new U.S. Navy full-pressure flying suit, a development of which is to be worn by the Project Mercury astronauts.

The U.S. machine, at the Aviation Acceleration Laboratory at Johnsville, Pennsylvania, has a 50-ft. arm driven by a 4,000-h.p. motor weighing 180 tons. On this the gondola can be rotated to simulate turns, dives and pull-outs of an aircraft.

These machines have assisted in the development of special clothing which enables remarkably high "g" loads to be sustained without harm.

The clothing automatically squeezes the wearer's legs and body if "g" loads are experienced, preventing the blood draining from the head and thus reducing the effect of the force.

Although these experiments were concerned initially with flight in ordinary aeroplanes, similar problems exist in space travel, so that the experience gained is directly hastening forward the day when men will be able to venture into space. For example, the violent acceleration that is likely to be experienced as a rocket carries a man into orbit will produce a force indistinguishable from the "g" loads produced in an aircraft pulling out of a steep dive. Experiments with centrifuges showed that a man can withstand higher "g" loads lying on his back than in any other position. It is not very easy to make use of this information where aircraft are con-

Short periods of weightlessness can be achieved by putting aircraft in what are called "ballistic" trajectories. This is a zoom climb and dive in which the occupants are able to fall freely under the influence of gravity and thus feel weightless.

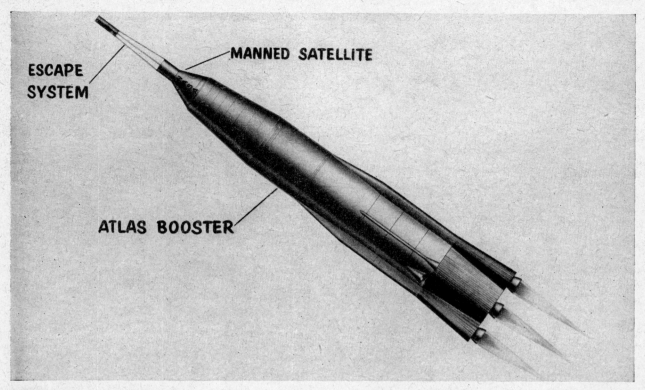

ESCAPE SYSTEM

MANNED SATELLITE

ATLAS BOOSTER

PROJECT MERCURY. One day soon a man will make the first journey through space. He may be an American or he may be a Russian. Little is known of the Russian plans, but the American programme has been given the code name of Project Mercury. The picture above shows how the astronaut will be lifted into orbit by a giant Atlas booster. Below is the tiny cabin in which the journey will be made. The occupant will lie on his back on a special couch.

cerned, but it is in the case of man-carrying rockets where the take-off will be entirely automatic and there will be no need for the pilot to see where he is going.

A pilot flying at 100,000 ft. is above 99% of the Earth's atmosphere—for many practical purposes he is in space. To ensure safe flight at these extreme altitudes special pressure-flying suits have been developed, to permit the wearers to bale out and descend safely to the lower altitudes where they can breathe normally. As their name indicates these suits can be pressurised in an emergency and are well on the way to the true space-suit of tomorrow. In fact, the space-suit to be worn by the American Project Mercury crews is only slightly different from the omni-environmental flying suit developed for U.S. Navy pilots.

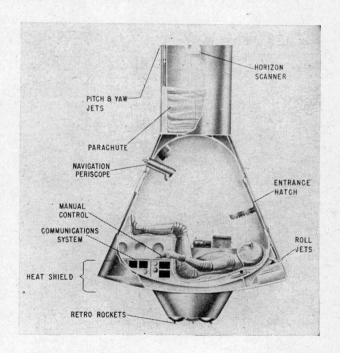

HORIZON SCANNER

PITCH & YAW JETS

PARACHUTE

NAVIGATION PERISCOPE

ENTRANCE HATCH

MANUAL CONTROL

COMMUNICATIONS SYSTEM

ROLL JETS

HEAT SHIELD

RETRO ROCKETS

189

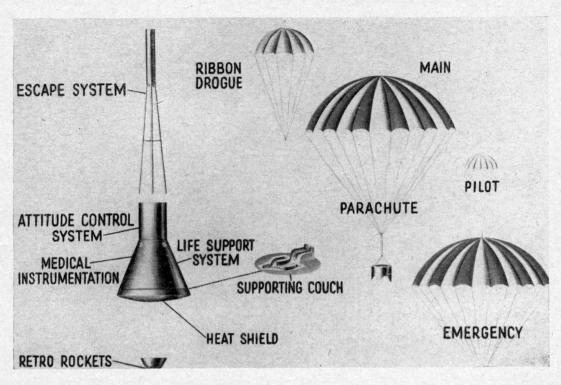

ESCAPE SYSTEM

RIBBON DROGUE

MAIN

ATTITUDE CONTROL SYSTEM

LIFE SUPPORT SYSTEM

MEDICAL INSTRUMENTATION

SUPPORTING COUCH

PARACHUTE

PILOT

HEAT SHIELD

EMERGENCY

RETRO ROCKETS

The Mercury man-carrying satellite and, below, the sequence of events during an orbital flight. The escape system rockets would pull the cabin away from the booster in an emergency. Normally, however, they would be jettisoned with the Atlas side motors soon after take-off, as shown.

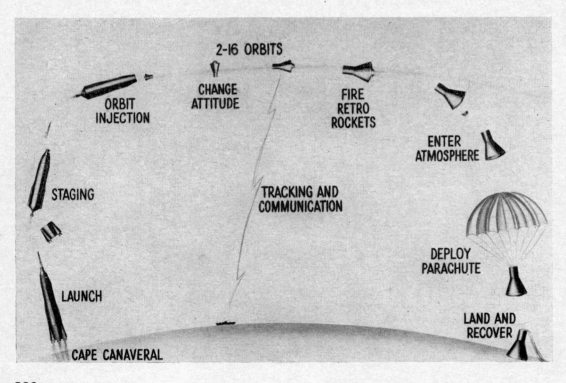

2-16 ORBITS

ORBIT INJECTION

CHANGE ATTITUDE

FIRE RETRO ROCKETS

ENTER ATMOSPHERE

STAGING

TRACKING AND COMMUNICATION

LAUNCH

DEPLOY PARACHUTE

CAPE CANAVERAL

LAND AND RECOVER

In addition to the practical difficulties and dangers of space, resulting from the lack of air and pressure and radiation, there will be the psychological factor of loneliness. The quiet emptiness, and utter vastness of space is going to impart a terrific sensation of loneliness. Strong nerves will be required for a man to withstand the sensation of total isolation. To try to gain advance information on whether a man will be able to keep fit under such conditions experiments have been made with a Space Cabin Simulator. Built at the Headquarters of the U.S. Aviation School of Medicine at Randolph Air Force Base, Texas, this is cunningly designed to make its occupant think he is in a space ship, in orbit. As previously explained, it is not possible to make the occupant feel weightless, as he would be in space, but in most other aspects the conditions duplicate those which would be experienced in a satellite orbiting the Earth 1,000 miles up.

Inside the cabin the air pressure is reduced to about half normal, equal to the air pressure at 18,000 ft., as space ships will be easier to design if the pressure can be reduced. The oxygen content, however, is twice the normal proportion, so the occupant breathes in as much oxygen as he would normally. As he breathes, the waste carbon dioxide exhaled is absorbed by chemicals. If it accumulated in the cabin he would suffocate.

It is replaced by fresh oxygen from the cabin's own self-contained supply, as it would be in the real thing. Excess heat given off by the occupant's body in the confined interior is reduced by special climatising equipment, before the temperature rises to an uncomfortable level. Occupants eat food in concentrated form, just as they would in space where every ounce of weight is precious.

Volunteers have spent up to a week in the simulator, long enough for a journey to the Moon and back. While the experiment is on, although the occupant is completely isolated from all noise and outside activities, he is

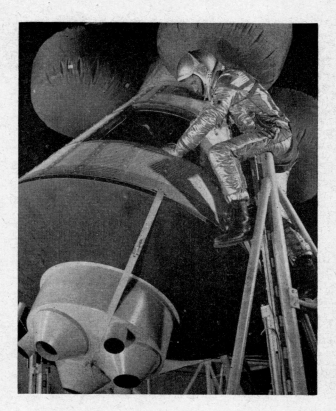

One of the seven Mercury astronauts, in his special pressure-suit, climbing aboard a mock-up of the capsule. At the top are the flotation bags to keep it afloat after a descent at sea. The retro-rockets are at the bottom.

constantly surveyed by a team of doctors and scientists by means of a T.V. camera. To see if the strain is affecting his mental alertness he is tested at intervals by an instrument panel that shows him patterns on a television-tube, which he has to match against charts inside the simulator. The results are studied after the experiment and provide a guide as to how long a person can keep functioning efficiently.

Great attempts are being made to try and obtain advance information on what the effect of weightlessness will be. This is one of the big unknowns of space flight. In everyday life we are weightless for a fraction of a second when a lift starts descending, and we all know the funny feeling that produces. In a coasting space ship it will be much worse and

One day before the end of the present century man will land on the Moon. It is too early yet to know what the space-ship used for the adventure will look like, but this is one suggestion by an artist of the Boeing Aerospace Division. Note that the space-ship's cabin detaches itself after landing, to become a vehicle for exploration of the surface of the Moon.

Long before this happens we shall know what the surface looks like and what it is made of, because plans are already being completed for landing pilotless rockets there, carrying packages of instruments, radio and even small tracked vehicles that will crawl over the surface and send back TV pictures.

will continue for days and weeks. So far, the best method developed involves the use of aircraft which are dived to the highest possible speed and then put into a "ballistic" trajectory. This means that they behave as does a thrown stone, or a shell the instant it leaves the gun barrel. For up to half a minute, during which the occupants are weightless, the aircraft arcs gracefully through the air, before the wings arrest the fall and normal weight returns.

The reactions of people taking part in these "weightless" experiments has been varied. Some have been violently sick, some have not been able to think clearly. Others, however, have almost come to enjoy it. Recently experiments have been made on what it is going to be like eating in space.

Here again, one realises how utterly different space will be to normal living. When you drink a cup of tea on Earth, the fluid flows from the cup into your mouth under the action of gravity. In space, if you turned the cup, nothing would happen, not even if you turned it right upside down. You would be able to move the cup away leaving the "ball" of tea suspended in mid air!

The solution to the drinking problem seems to be plastic bottles, which can be squeezed to force the liquid into the spaceman's mouth. Swallowing is largely a muscular action so that once the liquid is inside one's mouth no undue difficulties are expected, although attempts to eat some dry biscuits during a series of weightless hops were not too successful.

Since the satellites started circling the earth we now know there are layers of intense radiation extending for thousands of miles. At some heights the radiation intensity seems sufficient to present a real hazard to manned space flight.

But even if shielding has to be provided to protect man from these invisible rays, it will not prevent our conquering space. It will only cause delay. For our natural curiosity will ensure that, sooner or later, man will set out on the greatest adventure of all time.